Getting Others To Do What You Want

Lynne Franklin

Getting Others To Do What You Want

Copyright © 2014 by Lynne A. Franklin

ISBN 978-1-940170-51-0

To my family, who loved me through this process. To my friends, who believed in me. To my colleagues, who encouraged me. To my dog, Ralph, who slept nearby through most of this. And to my husband, who was never quite sure what I was up to but always had my back. Thanks for being in my life.

Table of Contents

Introduction

"Did you ever stop to think, and forget to start again?"
– A. A. Milne

This is not a book about manipulation. It's about awareness.

How many times have you thought, "If my people would just do what I tell them to, everything would be great!" Or "that client." Or "that business partner." Or "my family!"

One thing I can promise you—because I've been there—is that you were focused on yourself.

Did "Because I Said So!" *Ever* Work?

I believe that business leaders screw themselves over every day because they believe it's all about them. And it's not because we're narcissistic or power mad. It's because stress, anxiety and overwhelm make us small. We become reactive and defensive. In that moment, we can't distinguish the difference between *telling people what to do* and *getting them to do what we want.*

Do you remember being a teenager and asking your parents *why* you had to do your homework right now? How did it feel when they replied, "Because I *said* so!" I'm betting you felt motivated in that moment—but it wasn't to do what they *asked* …

Insisting on our way—for whatever reason—is us at our least powerful. No *wonder* we can't get others to do what we want!

The Message Trap

Many business leaders spend lots of time coming up with messages about what they want employees, current and potential clients, and investors to do. They practice their messages until these are polished to a sheen. And then they bask in the glow.

But they're wrong—and everyone suffers. And so do their companies' profits. And so do their opportunities for advancement.

Here's why. Leaders can be so focused on what *they want to say* that they really haven't any clue about *what the people they're trying to reach want to know*. They send forth these marvelous messages and are shocked when nothing happens.

How to Make Things Happen

This book offers a four-step mindset to use your smarts, your emotional intelligence, and the wonderful tool that's your brain to become more persuasive. I call these the "Four Gets"—the four things we too often forget under stress:

- *Step #1: Get Your Brain Back* – because, chances are, you have lost parts of your mind and need to have all your wits about you

- *Step #2: Get Clear on Your Goals* – how can you lead other people if you're not sure where you're going

- *Step #3: Get Persuasive* – it helps to know the process everyone's brain must go through in order to agree to do anything, so you can meet them where they are and take them to the next step

- *Step #4: Get Communicating* – with all of the other steps as background, you're finally ready to pick the right tactics that will actually reach people

In other words, this book is about developing an approach that gets people to say "yes" faster.

This Book Isn't for You If ...

Here's what you won't find here. There's no CEO bashing. No "employees are good and executives are unfeeling." No quick-fix-60-day program to better leadership. You already know that effective communication is a commitment: one you have to keep in mind every day—not a "one and done" check off the list item.

Still reading? Are you a business leader who's not sure you're doing everything you should? This is for you. Are you a CEO who is absolutely sure you're doing everything you need to communicate well? Then you *really* need this book.

But if you're a middle manager who is comfortable with staying there, then put down this book. The ideas here are only for people who are committed to playing big and getting—and practicing—the practical tools to do that.

This Stuff Works

I can help you only because I've already done this for a number of CEOs and CFOs these past 20+ years as a business communication consultant. They come to me because they need to communicate a merger with another company to their employees. They need to tell investors the truth about why the company fell short of financial guidance. They need to get money to expand their business when the company is showing a loss now. And they are willing to be honest not only about their strengths but what they didn't do well—and are open to trying something new.

If you're ready to lead a company that truly offers two-way communication so everyone can be more successful—and realize this starts with you—then read on. I promise you'll get information you can use right away that will make a positive difference.

Be the leader you've always wanted to be. Your company, clients employees, investors—and family—are waiting.

Why Wait for *Your* Reward?

Let's have fun!

Because you've invested in yourself by getting this book, you deserve it.

Go to my website—www.yourwordsmith.com—and download your gift: *Something Funny about Business Communication: 12 Oddball Theories and 38 Tips for Getting What You Want on the Job.*

This is a collection of some of my favorite communication theories created over the years. These draw from the foibles of the people around me—such as "The Hydrant Theory"—as well as my own mistakes—"The Words Make Bad Lovers Theory."

They are designed to give you more than a chuckle. You'll also get actions you can take right away to keep your sanity and take charge of a situation.

If you like this gift, then you may enjoy the place it comes from: my *In Communicado* e-newsletter. Every month, you get my wry view on neuroscience and communication—and nothing else (I promise never to share your contact information). And check out the archives for other useful subjects.

Now, on to getting others to do what you want!

It All Started with Fred

"I don't look at a knife the way I used to.
I'm more aware of what it is. I think twice."
– Neil Young

Fred is a fourteen-year-old boy standing three feet in front of me. If you ask me what he looks like, in this moment I couldn't tell you. His right arm is slightly raised, and all I can see is that he is holding the world's largest machete. It has a black plastic handle and a wide gleaming silver blade that tapers to a wicked sharp point.

"If you try to call for help, I'm going to cut you, bitch!" he growls.

I think to myself, "How the heck did I get here?"

I am the only adult in the boys' group home that afternoon. Fred and I are standing in the staff office of Daniel Cottage. There is a cluster of four teenage boys in the hallway behind Fred. They're almost fizzing with nerves, getting squirrely over the prospect that Fred might knife me. "Fred, my man," calls one. "Gonna cut *Staff* to the *bone!*"

Sweat has turned the back of my shirt into a Rorschach test. (The answer is "fear!") But my brain *still* hasn't caught up with the situation. I'm thinking, "All I asked Fred to do was go to the Intake Department, so they could talk with him about what he's been up to since running away from Daniel Cottage two days ago. If he'd just do what I tell him, everything would be fine."

Then Fred brings down the knife with a *swoosh!* and cuts the cord between the phone and the wall. The phone I had picked up to call for backup, so someone else could be with the other boys while I worked with Fred to get him to Intake.

I have just lost my mind.

11

What I'm *not* thinking about is what *Fred* is thinking about, which is, "I'm tired of adults always telling me what to do, and I've had *enough!*"

I start tap-dancing in my head. All I can think of to do is babble. "But Fred—I *like* you! And you like me. You don't really want to hurt me." Even I can hear the pleading tone in my voice.

Fred's narrowed eyes, clenched teeth, and the raised machete show that he is *not* buying this.

So I keep babbling. "And you don't want to get into the world of hurt you're going to get into if you hurt me."

That's when he blinks. Now I'm talking about things from *his* perspective. I am taking him into a future where he has stabbed me. Daniel Cottage will no longer be his home. The boys in the hallway will no longer be his friends. I won't be there to help him. The police will come and drag his butt off to juvenile hall. Then he'll go to court. And he'll probably be locked up in some institution.

His eyes—which had been locked in a glare at mine—drop for an instant. Fred's right arm—the one holding the knife—trembles.

This is my chance.

So I stick out my right hand. "Let's make this easy on you, Fred," I say. "Just hand me the knife so I can lock it up."

I'm not sure how much time passes, but these are some of the longest minutes of my life. I am afraid he will bring the knife down and cut my outstretched hand. But I know I have to keep it out there. Fred needs to see that I trust him not to cut me. That I believe he is a good kid. Then he can *act* like one.

Fred finally looks down for a moment, takes a deep breath and lowers his arm. I reach out and he lets me take the knife.

"Thanks, Fred," I say. I open the locked cabinet in the office and place the machete inside. When I hear the closing "click" of the lock, I shut my eyes in relief and lean my palms briefly against the cabinet, taking a deep breath and trying to regain some energy and composure before turning around.

Then I look past Fred to the other boys and say, "OK: show's over. Don't you have something else to do besides hang out in the hallway? If you don't, I'll be happy to *find* something for you. Fred and I need to talk."

I'm sure the boys who liked me were glad to see that I didn't get hurt. I'm also sure some of the others are sorry the drama is over and there has been no blood. All of them melt away—because no one wants to do any of the chores I would give them.

"So Fred," I say, "sit down here and tell me what's going on."

His brown body drops into the chair behind him. His dirty red T-shirt and cut-off jeans hang from his skinny frame. There isn't a menacing bone in his body now—and it's almost hard to believe I was so afraid of him a minute ago.

That's when he tells me where he was for the last two days when he was "on run." He went to see his mother—whom I know is a schizophrenic.

"Every time I'd be in the house, she'd be telling me to go outside and play," he says, his voice cracking. "And then I'd be outside, and she'd be hollering at me to come back in. And when I'd be watching TV, she'd be telling me to get the hell back in my room or she'd mess me up. I always do what she be telling me, but she ain't *never* happy."

He had taken the knife from a closet at home: first, to make sure his mother wouldn't use it on him, and second, to protect himself if she came at him.

This was the moment that the Daniel Cottage social worker and unit supervisor burst into the office. People had been trying to reach us for the last half hour, but the phone just kept ringing. They were surprised to hear why ...

Here's what I didn't know until a long time later. While I hadn't created this situation, there were things I did—or didn't do—that made it worse. There also is a four-step process I could have used so Fred would have given me the knife much sooner than he did—and both of us would have suffered a lot less.

I know it's unlikely that someone will come into your office or home wielding a machete and threatening to kill you. (Unless you work at a children's home—for which you have my undying admiration!) What I learned since Fred is what I want to share with you here, to prevent you from dying—literally and figuratively—by getting other people to do what you want.

These are the Four "Gets": the four things we forget when we're under stress. Let's make them work for you.

Get Your Brain Back

"To *know* something, you need to *know* something."
– Zarm Geisenhoff

Have you ever looked around and thought, "This situation is out of control!" Maybe you just discovered a case of fraud at your company—and all of the profit it made last year has evaporated in an instant. Perhaps you find illegal drugs in your teenager's room. Or you get a notice that your checking account has been cleaned out and that you're the victim of identity theft. Suddenly, what you thought was the solid world around you evaporates. Everything is moving in slow motion—and you feel as though you've lost your mind.

I certainly did with Fred, while I was standing there babbling and afraid I was going to die.

This really *does* happen. To know why and what to do about it, let's take a quick trip through some practical neuroscience.

OK: I'm a neuroscience nerd. I love studying how the brain works and how that affects our choices and behavior. While I'm as much of a theory wonk as the next person, if I can't put what I learn to work, I don't have too much use for it. Now on to the useful stuff.

Your Three Brains

There are three parts to your brain.

Your *survival brain* is the oldest. It's in charge of two things: keeping your body running and keeping you alive. Not a lot of thinking goes on here. You basically have three choices: fight, flight or freeze.

Your *emotional brain* is the place where your feelings live. You generally have five choices here: mad, sad, glad, hurt and afraid.

Your *thinking brain* collects information from your survival and emotional brains—which aren't aware of each other. Its job is to analyze this information and then make practical, smart and ethical decisions.

These three brains layer on top of each other—and all three are always there.

Triune Brain

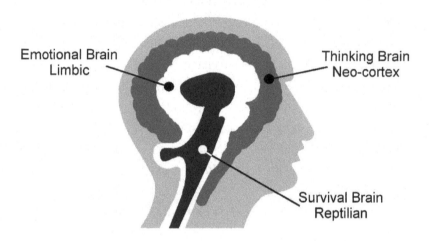

Emotional Brain
Limbic

Thinking Brain
Neo-cortex

Survival Brain
Reptilian

Your Three Brains in Crisis

In a crisis, you literally lose two-thirds of your brain: your thinking and emotional brains leave town. All you have left is your survival brain. It's logical to wonder why you would lose the bulk of your brain when it appears you need it the most. Here's how I explain this.

In the old-old days, when we were living in the jungle, you see a fast-moving object coming toward you. If your thinking brain were in charge, it would be asking, "What *is* this thing coming toward me?" It would be analyzing the image. Because "it" happened to be a tiger—*wham!* you'd be dead.

If your emotional brain were in charge, you'd be asking yourself, "How do I *feel* about this thing coming toward me?" And—*wham!* you'd be dead.

Because your survival brain is in charge, it notices the threat before your other two brains do. It already has you up the tree. And—*whew!* you'd be alive.

When you're really frightened, your body diverts impulses from the thinking and emotional brains to a particular part of your survival brain, called the amygdala. The amygdala is in charge of scanning your environment for physical and verbal threats. When it perceives these, the amygdala takes over. I love the term for this: "amygdala hijack."

In other words, your amygdala shuts down your other two brains. You lose your emotional intelligence. Stress hormones (epinephrine and cortisol) flood your system. Epinephrine raises your heart rate—so your body can move more blood to the large muscle groups that may need it for fight or flight. It also dilates your pupils—which lets more light into your eyes so you can see better.

Cortisol puts a damper on your immune system—which reduces any inflammation you'll suffer if you're wounded. It also gets your brain stem to stimulate your amygdala even more—which, in turn, produces more cortisol. Now there's enough cortisol in your system to suppress your hippocampus—which usually is in charge of putting the brakes on your amygdala. Not surprisingly, your ability to make logical choices drops drastically, and your working memory falters.

You can't reason with someone—including yourself—when you're in amygdala hijack. That's where Fred and I were, standing three feet from each other, when he had his knife raised.

What you need to know now is how to get your brain back.

Reclaim Your Brain

While every crisis feels different to you, they all go through the same stages.

The best description I've found to get through this situation comes from psychiatrist Mark Goulston.[1] He calls this the "Oh F#@& To OK" process. Here's a user's guide to get through it.

Reaction Phase

This is where I was as soon as Fred cut the phone cord, after I made it past the denial part: "If he'd just go to Intake, everything would be fine." Right now I'm in panic mode. What's going through my mind is, "I am so screwed! He's going to kill me!"

How to Get Through It: I was literally in my survival brain, with its three choices of fight, flight or freeze. The first thing I *should* have done was name my feeling—which was fear. And, considering the environment, I should have done this in my head. Saying "I'm afraid" out loud—in front of Fred and all of the boys—probably would have further destabilized the situation. I was the adult and supposed to be in charge. Had they known I was afraid, everyone's anxiety level probably would have hit the ceiling. On the other hand, denying to *myself* that I was afraid meant wasting a lot of my energy trying to convince myself of something I knew wasn't true.

Because I wasn't sure what was going to happen next, I was holding my breath. It would have helped to exhale and breathe deeply. Depending upon where you are, close your eyes. This limits your outside stimulation and can help to calm your mind.

Why This Works: There's a helpful line: "Name it to tame it." Once you're not denying your feeling—because you've named it—you start to move into your emotional brain. At least that gets you from three choices (fight, flight or freeze) to five (mad, sad, glad, hurt and afraid).

---

[1] Goulston, Mark. *Just Listen: Discover the Secret to Getting Through to Absolutely Everyone.* AMACOM 2010.

Release Phase

If you're like me, at this moment you'd love it if someone would come in and save you from whatever mess you're in. In this second phase, you realize that isn't going to happen. But you're still feeling a little victim-y about it.

With Fred standing there, I'm thinking, "How the heck did I get here? The cavalry isn't going to ride to my rescue. I'm going to have to save myself."

How to Get Through It: It would have helped if I had continued to breathe deeply through my nose. Once again, because I was with the boys, there was no way to close my eyes—who knows what mayhem might have erupted if I wasn't watching? But if you can, it's still good to limit some of that information coming through your dilated pupils.

Why This Works: The idea is to take that pause you require to regain your inner balance. You need the chance to calm your body—with all of those stress hormones rushing through it. Go ahead: feel a bit sorry for yourself—heaven knows *I* did! But take this time to get your balance back.

Recenter Phase

I never really got here with Fred. I was just babbling about liking him and him liking me. This was me literally buying time until I could figure out what to do, trying to fill the silence, and calm *myself* as much as him.

How to Get Through It: Now I know I should have kept breathing (besides the shallow gulps of air I was taking between my ramblings). It would have helped me to keep saying to myself, "This is scary, but I can deal with it."

Why This Works: I view this as the equivalent of a 12-Step program, such as Alcoholics Anonymous. Each action step is preceded by one that *prepares* you. For example, Step #8 is "Made a list of all people we had harmed, and became willing to make amends to them all." Then #9 is "Made direct amends to such people wherever possible, except when to do so would injure them or others."

This phase is where you gather your wits and your confidence, which will propel you through the rest of the process.

Refocus Phase

I didn't get here, either. What I got was lucky. In my verbal wanderings, I hit upon the idea, "And you don't want to get into the world of hurt you'll get into if you hurt me." This was something that actually connected with Fred.

How to Get Through It: Now you're ready to be on your own side. And in your mind, you speak this to yourself. "I will *not* let this ruin my career, my relationship, my day, my life," my whatever. Follow that with "Here is what I need to do *right now* to make it better."

The "right now" is important. If you're like me, you can project yourself so far down the future that you miss the present. This kind of stuff can paralyze you. It can make the problem so big that you feel overwhelmed—not a good choice in this moment! Stick with what you need to get through the next five minutes (in my case with Fred) rather than the next month. There will be time to figure out the other stuff later.

Why It Works: Because you've gone through the other three phases, you now have your thinking brain back. This means you are physiologically able to start considering what you can do to limit the damage and make the best of the situation you face.

Reengaging Phase

I got to this stage with Fred on sheer intuition. After seeing him blink and the knife waver—and hearing my gut tell me this was my chance—I asked for the knife and stuck out my hand to take it. And I can't overestimate how lucky I was that he accepted my invitation.

How to Get Through It: You have reached the point where you can say to yourself, "I'm ready to handle this." And you'll be right. If you've had your eyes closed until now, you can open them and see more than disaster. You can understand why, in Chinese, the character for "crisis" is the combination of two others: "danger" and "opportunity."

Why It Works: You have allowed your brain to go through all of the stages it needs to recover from amygdala hijack. Plus you have done this without short-shrifting yourself emotionally, which would have happened if you had denied your feelings and pretended that you weren't afraid—as in my case with Fred. Or hurt. Or sad. Or angry. (I'm betting that you will never lose your mind because you're so happy!)

Now That You *Know* Something ...

Often we go through crises because we're focused on how the world *should* be, but *isn't*—and probably never will be. I thought Fred should just go to Intake. He thought adults shouldn't tell him what to do. The process of getting our brains back prepares us to deal with the world as it *is*.

It may take a while to train your brain to go through all of these steps—because, after all, you've lost your mind! But with practice, you can reduce the amount of time it takes to move through this. Some people can do it in only a few minutes. But if you've been stuck at a phase in times past—the "why does this happen to me?" victimhood of the Release Phase has been a traditional favorite of mine—you now know how you may move past it.

Just as important is the knowledge that your family, friends, clients, and even the stranger who cuts in front of you on the highway can be doing this because *they* are going through amygdala hijack. When they, like Fred, are stuck in the Reaction Phase, you may see all kinds of aggression they use to mask their fear, hurt and sadness. Often this shows up as strident, vein-pulsing anger, because they are literally scared out of *their* minds. Other people may react with tears.

Now you know they are in their survival brains. It may be your job—or your gift to them—to help them get *their* brains back. It all starts with

21

that simple question, "What are you feeling?" If I had been wise enough to ask that of Fred, it would have saved a lot of wear and tear on both of us.

- You have three brains:
  1. Your survival brain keeps your body running and alive. You have three choices here: fight, flight or freeze.
  2. Your emotional brain contains all of your feelings. You have five choices here: mad, sad, glad, hurt and afraid.
  3. Your thinking brain houses all of your higher analytical powers and is aware of what's happening in your other two brains.

- You lose two-thirds of your mind when in crisis. All you have left is your survival brain. The part of it that's in charge is called the amygdala. It overrides everything else when it senses a physical or verbal threat.

- You can get your brain back by following Mark Goulston's "Oh F#@& To OK" process:
  1. *Reaction Phase:* You think all is lost and your only three options are fight, flight or freeze. Start engaging your emotional brain by asking, "What am I feeling?"
  2. *Release Phase:* While you wish someone would come in and save you, you understand this won't happen. Breathe deeply and admit that you're going to have to do this yourself.
  3. *Recenter Phase:* Keep breathing and know that you have the resources to deal with this. Now you're starting to get your thinking brain back.
  4. *Refocus Phase:* This is where you combine your emotional and thinking brain, using anger on your own behalf by saying to yourself, "I'm not going to let this ruin my life!"
  5. *Reengaging Phase:* Your thinking brain is back in full force, and you're ready to start strategizing on what you can do immediately to deal with the situation.

Learn from Your Past

1. Remember a chaotic situation when it felt as though you had lost your mind:

    a. Where and when did this take place?

    _____

    _____

    b. What happened?

    _____

    _____

    c. What were you doing?

    _____

    _____

    d. Who else was involved?

    _____

    _____

2. Now consider what you would do differently if this happened today by applying the five phases:

a. Reaction Phase – how would you get past "I'm screwed!"?

_____

_____

b. Release Phase – how do you move beyond your wish to be rescued?

_____

_____

c. Recenter Phase – what resources do you have to handle this situation?

_____

_____

d. Refocus Phase – what won't you let this situation ruin for you?

_____

_____

e. Reengaging Phase – what will you do to start making things better in the next few minutes?

_____

_____

3. How is this different from what actually happened?

_____

_____

Prepare for the Future Exercise

1. List some of the events you are afraid might escalate into a crisis.

_____

_____

2. Close your eyes and place yourself in one of those situations.
3. Ask yourself, "What am I feeling?"
4. What will you do after this?

_____

_____

Get Clear on Your Goals

"People with clear, written goals, accomplish far more
in a shorter period of time than people without them
could ever imagine."
– Brian Tracy

Now that we have our brains back, we can move on to the second of the "Four Gets."

Fred and I were both stuck in our self-centered goals. Fred was tired of adults who looked right through him and told him what to do. His goal was not to take this anymore. I was in trouble because my focus on getting Fred to go to the Intake Department meant I wasn't paying attention to what was happening with him.

The situation clearly called for me to change my goal. First, to not dying! Second, to making sure no one else did. Suddenly things became very simple, and I could see how unimportant getting Fred to go to Intake was in the scheme of things.

But here's the truth for us in business. Nearly every minute at the office we're confronted with opportunities to succeed or fail—and we sleepwalk through many of them because we don't set goals.

Bring Out the Blowtorch

Once I was working with a CEO on the text for his annual report to shareholders. He and I were scheduled to meet on Monday morning to discuss it. His assistant Rachel called to let me know that his flight had been delayed by bad weather and that our meeting needed to be pushed back until late that afternoon.

Then she added, "He's in a really bad mood. The weather was awful all weekend and he didn't get the chance to relax and go sailing. He said he wants to torch your annual report copy."

Now *that's* a meeting I really want to go to.

My traditional approach would have been to have a low-grade sense of dread in the back of my head all day about this meeting. I would have tried to soothe myself a bit by saying, "I've handled clients in a bad mood before, so I certainly can deal with him." Then I would have proceeded to go into the meeting and wing it. Chances are good that it would have gone something like this:

"Hi John. I was sorry to hear that the weather was bad for you this weekend."

"That's not the only thing that's bad. This shareholders' letter is the worst thing I've ever read! It's nothing like what I told you I wanted to have in it. What you wrote is terrible and I'm not going to pay you anything for this."

Can you feel an amygdala hijack coming on? I can. Not only am I defensive, I'm also worried about not getting paid! I will likely spend all of my energy tap dancing around what to say next—just the way I did with Fred. That means I probably won't hear everything John has to say, which will further infuriate him. I've drastically reduced the chances that this will turn out well for *either* of us.

Instead of spending the next few hours fretting—and probably not getting any other work done—I sat down and wrote my goals for this meeting:

1. Let John blow off steam.
2. Help him feel seen and heard.
3. Stick up for myself: explain rather than defend.
4. Find out what the specific issues are so I can fix them.
5. Come away with a plan on what to do next.

I would bring the sheet of paper with me, read it in the car, take a deep breath and put it down on the passenger seat before entering the building.

After finishing my list, I looked up at a shelf above my desk. On it, there was a working blowtorch made of polished brass. My husband purchased it for me years ago, because I was fond of saying, "The only way my desk will *ever* be clear is if I use a blowtorch on it!" There have been times of great disarray when I have taken it down, pointed it at my desk, and made blowtorch combustion sounds.

I decided to take a risk.

When John walked through the conference room door, the expression on his face was every bit as stormy as I imagined the weather had been for him that weekend. The sheaf of marked up annual report text was slightly crumpled in his left hand.

"Hi John," I said, rising. "Rachel told me that you felt like 'torching the annual report copy.' As your consultant, it's my job to help you get what you want. Here you go!" I lifted the blowtorch from the table and held it out for him.

John stopped and glowered at the blowtorch. I was afraid I'd made a miscalculation with him. Then there was a slow smile. He put down the papers and took the blowtorch.

For the next 10 minutes, he told me how, as a young man, he had bought an old wooden Chris-Craft runabout. Then he spent the summer renovating it. This included using a blowtorch to remove the barnacles and old varnish on the hull, so he could sand, re-stain and varnish it. He even showed me the proper way to light the torch.

John was now visibly relaxed. After saying, "This is a really nice blowtorch!" he was ready to move on to the report.

The funny thing was, his changes were relatively minor. I was able to leave the meeting with a clear direction on the revisions, and he left it having relived a pleasant memory with an attentive audience. All because I had taken 30 seconds to write my goals and saw that blowtorch on the shelf!

Do-It-Yourself Business Communication Goals

Setting at least one goal allows you to do two valuable things before you speak with or write to anyone. First, it helps you develop messages that will connect with the people you want to reach. You can do this by answering two simple but powerful questions:

1. What's my point?
2. Why does it matter?

Second, it helps you better prepare to deliver those messages—and handle any questions or objections that arise in the process.

To get you started, it might be useful to know the five basic functions of business communication. You may work these into your goals if any of them apply:

1. *Inform* – to share information
2. *Request* – ask for something
3. *Record* – tell people about a meeting or event that has already happened
4. *Instruct* – tell people how to do something
5. *Persuade* – get people to take action, which I believe is the purpose of *all* communication

Even setting goals around these simple concepts will help you become more effective.

Here's another idea. Think SMART goals:

Specific: A goal is much more powerful when it's clear. To say, "I make $150,000 in salary and $50,000 in bonuses this year" is more motivating than "I make more money." Would making $2 more this year than last *really* satisfy you?

Measurable: The same example works for this one. You will know if you reach $200,000.

Attainable: When you set a goal so high you know you can't reach it, this *de*motivates you. Studies show that people who set *no* goals actually do better than those who set *unrealistic* ones.

Relevant: I could have set a goal that John would compliment me on my new haircut during the meeting. This would have met the first three criteria (specific, measurable and attainable) but it certainly wouldn't have anything to do with what needs to be accomplished. Of course that's a silly example. But now that relevance is a part of your goal-setting mindset, you'll start noticing how many times people set goals that really aren't.

Timely: Having a deadline creates a sense of urgency—something that's lacking in Snow White's goal of "Some day my prince will come." It also gives you a sense of responsibility for making things happen and supports developing tactics and timelines to achieve it.

Your Brain on Goals

You *knew* I'd get back to neuroscience, didn't you?

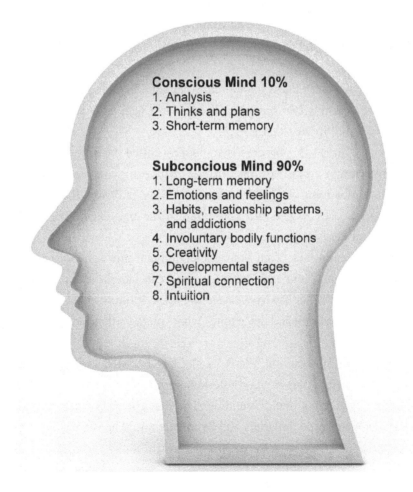

Conscious Mind 10%
1. Analysis
2. Thinks and plans
3. Short-term memory

Subconcious Mind 90%
1. Long-term memory
2. Emotions and feelings
3. Habits, relationship patterns, and addictions
4. Involuntary bodily functions
5. Creativity
6. Developmental stages
7. Spiritual connection
8. Intuition

You have three brains. Did you know you also have two minds? (What's the difference? I like Rick Hanson's definition: "The mind *is* what the brain *does*."[2] [The italics are mine.]) These are your conscious and subconscious minds. The graphic on the prior page offers a helpful distinction.

As you can see, your conscious mind is your thinking brain. You know what's going on here—and now you know how little that is in the larger playground of your mind! Your subconscious is part of your emotional brain and all of your survival brain—which, once again, coexist but aren't aware of each other. Here's the cool thing. When you set goals, you get both of your minds working together *for* you.

Why You Should Care about Your Reticular Activating System

While we don't know a lot about what's going on in our subconscious mind, we do know two things: 1) it wants us to get what we want, and 2) we have to tell it what that is.

What governs this process is something called the reticular activating system (RAS). This is the bridge between your conscious and subconscious minds. That's because it's the pathway that nearly all information uses to get into your brain. (The one exception is smells. These go directly to your emotional brain.)

Here's a fun fact. Your conscious mind can process about 40 bits of data per second. Your subconscious mind can handle 40 *million* bits of data per second! That's why we need the RAS. It filters all the information that enters your brain and determines what you pay attention to—and what you screen out.

Biologically speaking, the RAS is a loose confederation of nuclei in your brain stem—part of your emotional brain. There are two sections in the RAS: ascending and descending. The first connects with the thinking brain, as well as the thalamus and hypothalamus. The second links to the

---

[2] Hanson, Rick; Mendius, Richard. *Buddha's Brain*. New Harbinger Publications, Inc. 2009. Page 11.

cerebellum and the other four senses. This means it also plays an important role in breathing, sleeping, waking and your heartbeat.

As a gatekeeper, the RAS is more active during the day than at night. However, it also is connected to your ability to dream.

What does this have to do with getting clear on your goals? You can't do it without the RAS.

If I were to tell you, "Don't think about a red corvette," what are you thinking about? Right! That's because—suddenly—your RAS understands that a red corvette is important to you. For the rest of this week, you probably will be surprised by the number of red corvettes you see. While they were there all along, your RAS didn't know these cars were important to you, so it didn't bring them to your attention.

Chances are that you have experienced your RAS in other ways. Let's say that you're an Alfred Hitchcock film buff. Last night you watched one of your favorites: "North by Northwest." Tonight, you're at a networking event with other business leaders. The room is filled with conversations. You're enjoying one with the head of human resources at a health care company. From behind you, you hear, "I'm trying to remember who played the villain in that movie 'North by Northwest.'" You turn around and say, "That was James Mason." Then you return to your conversation.

How did you happen to hear *that* question among all of the buzz in this room? It's because your RAS was already tuned in to that movie title, so when someone spoke it, the RAS that let it through to your conscious mind.

Your RAS responds to two types of information: novelty and repetition. We're particularly interested in the latter here.

Setting goals gets your conscious and subconscious minds working together to help you get what you want. You literally have to tell your RAS what this is—by writing or speaking your goals, and repeating them. Then it goes to work, monitoring those millions of bits of data per second to find the people, articles, TV programs and other resources that will help you get there. And—miraculously—all of these start showing up in your life!

Maybe this has happened to you, too. I've gone to bed thinking about an issue or asking myself a question: "What can I do to get that potential client—who has been sitting on my proposal for two weeks—to work with me?" Often I'll wake up in the middle of the night, or the next morning, with an answer or strategy to use. "I'll call and say, 'Something is preventing you from saying "yes" to working with me. If you tell me what it is, I'll try to find a way to get you what you need so we can get started.'" That's because my RAS and subconscious have been "chewing" on it all night while I've been sleeping. These ideas always feel like such a gift!

Here's the important thing to remember about the RAS. It can't tell the difference between a *positive* and a *negative* message. This is best embodied by the Henry Ford quote: "Whether you think you can or you think you can't, you're right."

Have you ever struggled with a proposal or memo and thought, "They'll *never* sign off on this idea!" Guess what? Your RAS heard "never sign off on this idea" and is working hard to make sure you use words, tactics and strategies so that happens. Be *careful* what you feed your RAS!

Your RAS and Goal Setting

Whether or not you believe in the law of attraction, your RAS does.

It turns out that the Harvard 1979 and Yale 1953 studies of the importance of written goals were both urban myths. However, Dominican University took up the gauntlet in 2013.[3]

Dr. Gail Matthews did a month-long goal study, which was completed by 149 people. They ranged in age from 23 to 72, with 37 men and 112 women. Participants came from Australia, Belgium, England, India, Japan and the U.S. Their professions included entrepreneurs, educators, healthcare professionals, artists, attorneys, bankers, marketers, human services providers, managers, vice presidents and directors of not-for-profits.

These people were divided into five groups:

---

[3] Matthews, Gail. Dominican University. Viewed at http://www.dominican.edu/academics/ahss/undergraduate-programs-1/psych/faculty/fulltime/gailmatthews/researchsummary2.pdf on March 22, 2014.

1. *Group 1:* Thought about a goal and then rated it on these dimensions: a) difficulty, b) importance, c) the extent to which they had the skills and resources to accomplish the goal, d) their commitment and motivation to reach the goal, e) whether or not they had pursued this goal in the past, and f) their level of success if they had worked toward the goal before
2. *Group 2:* Same as Group 1 but also wrote the goal (into an online survey)
3. *Group 3:* Same as Group 2 but also developed action commitments to reach the goal
4. *Group 4:* Same as Group 3 but also sent their goals and action commitments to a supportive friend
5. *Group 5:* Same as Group 4 but also sent weekly progress reports to a supportive friend

Just *thinking* about their goals helped 43% of the people in Group 1 achieve them. I say that's a strong vote for the RAS! Of course the other groups did better, with Group 2 at 61%, Group 3 at 51%, Group 4 at 64% and Group 5 at 76%.

Imagine how powerful this could be in your daily life. You can't expect your RAS to take you where you want to go unless you're clear on this—let alone where it could take your people. Start with the small stuff. What do you want to get out of your next meeting? Your next phone conversation? Your next email? That difficult conversation you've been putting off with your spouse or child? Doing this will help you find your *own* blowtorch!

- When we don't set goals in our daily lives, we have a tendency to sleepwalk through them and miss opportunities to get what we want.

- When setting goals around persuasive communications, it's useful to ask two questions:
  1. What's my point?
  2. Why does it matter?

- There are five functions of business communication: inform, request, record, instruct and persuade.

- People are more successful with goal-setting when they use the SMART approach, making their goals specific, measurable, attainable, relevant and timely.

- Your conscious mind accounts for about 10% of your mental activity (analyzing, thinking and planning, and short-term memory), while your subconscious mind houses everything else.

- Your reticular activating system is the literal bridge between your conscious and subconscious minds. It sifts through the 40 million bits of information your brain captures every second and brings the relevant ones to your attention. This makes it important in setting goals.

- Your subconscious mind wants you to get what you want, but you literally have to tell it. At the same time, your subconscious mind can't discriminate between positive and negative messages, so be careful what you focus on.

What to Do Now

Immediate Gratification Goal Setting Exercise

1. Start with small goals. On the lines below, write at least one communication you'll do at the office tomorrow: from an important phone call to a meeting with people who report to you.

_____

_____

2. Write the answers to these two questions:
   a. What's my point?

_____

_____

   b. Why does it matter?

_____

_____

3. Write one goal using the SMART template: specific, measurable, attainable, relevant and timely.

_____

_____

4. Review your goal sheet before you do the communication.
5. Afterward, record how many goals you met.

---

6. How was this different from the last time you did something similar *without* setting a goal beforehand?

---

7. Each day, set goals for one or more business or personal situations and monitor your success rate.

Conundrum-Breaking Goal Setting Exercise

1. Before going to bed tonight, think of a problem that has been concerning or troubling you.
2. Close your eyes and take a deep breath.
3. Ask yourself, "What can I do tomorrow that will help me with this [problem]?"
4. Or say to yourself, "I want to [state your goal]. Help me find ways to do this."
5. Take another deep breath, then relax and go to sleep.
6. The next morning—or if you wake up in the middle of the night—record any ideas that come to you.
7. Determine which ones you want to try. Note how successful they are.

Get Persuasive

"The truth isn't the truth until people believe you. And they can't believe you if they don't know what you're saying. And they can't know what you're saying if they don't listen to you. And they won't listen to you if you're not interesting. And you won't be interesting until you say things imaginatively, originally, freshly."
– William Bernbach

Our first two "gets" were focused on us: getting our brains back and understanding what we really want by having clear goals. Now it's time to move on to the people we need to reach.

I wasn't able to do that with Fred. Being so focused on getting him to go to the Intake Department, I wasn't paying any attention to where he was in the process of being persuaded, which—as you're about to see—was resisting. If I had even stopped to say, "Tell me what's going on, Fred" and listened, I wouldn't have stood there, sweating, for 20 minutes. Fred would have seen that he had my attention, which is what he wanted anyway. He wouldn't have been so angry, and I wouldn't have been so afraid.

You can avoid that unnecessary drama by understanding the Persuasion Cycle. This was developed by Mark Goulston[4], based on the work of Carlo DiClemente and James Prochaska, authors of *Transtheoretical Model of Change*, and by William Miller and Stephen Rollnick, who co-wrote *Motivational Interviewing.*

---

[4] Goulston, op.cit., pages 8-10.

The Persuasion Cycle

This is one of the most powerful communication ideas I've ever come across. These are the steps our brains need to go through to agree to do anything.

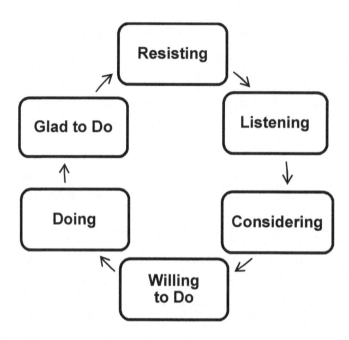

How My Screw Up Proved the Cycle Works

I started my corporate communications practice 20-some years ago. My first mistake, of course, was not having any sales training or having set up a system for doing sales. Since I needed more clients, it was time to make cold calls. (Does that term make *your* palms sweat? Mine are damp just remembering it!)

I thought the purpose of doing a cold call was to get a new client. The folly of this is clear now. I believed I could have a five-minute phone conversation and magically transport a person from *resisting* to *willing to do*. How successful was I? I stank. Here's how the Persuasion Cycle has helped me put the new business process in context:

1. The purpose of a cold call is to have a conversation—to move from *resisting* to *listening.*
2. The purpose of a conversation is to set a meeting—to move from *listening* to *considering.*
3. The purpose of a meeting is to get permission to submit a proposal—to move from *considering* to *willing to do.*
4. The purpose of a proposal is to get the business—to move from *willing to do* to *doing.*

Then it's my job to do the work so well that my clients are *glad to do* and *willing to do again.* And when that's the case, I can move them through the front part of the cycle—from resisting to considering—much faster next time.

Here's one of the blessings of understanding the Persuasion Cycle. Now I know quantum leaps aren't required: I don't *have* to move people from resisting to willing to do in one grand motion. I just need to make incremental progress with each communication. That certainly reduces my angst—and resistance to taking action—and increases the chances I'll set realistic goals and actually meet them.

Paying Attention to Buy-In

Our focus in this chapter is the front end of the cycle: resisting, listening and considering. There are two reasons for this.

First, these are the steps where we create buy-in from the people we're trying to persuade. If we don't accomplish this, we'll never have a shot at the rest of the process of getting them to do what we want. That makes it crucial to get this right.

Maybe you have been in this situation. You pitched someone on an idea and then created a proposal. Then you met with her, thinking she's ready to sign off on your ideas. She glanced through what you gave her and said, "This is all well and good, but I need a few more days to think about it." She had buyer's remorse. You have just experienced a breakdown somewhere between considering and willing to do—so you have to backtrack through listening and considering. It makes sense to focus on ways to avoid this.

Second, I believe this is the hardest part of the process for most of us. If you're spending the time to read this book, you're probably passionate about what you and your company do, or about making a difference at home or at the office. This likely means that, given the opportunity to share your passion, you can be pretty convincing—and do a good job of handling willing to do, doing, and glad to do. Let's work on the tools that get you to that opportunity.

Resisting

Even people who agree with you and *want* to say "yes" will resist you. The good news is that this has nothing to do with you—it's just how our brains are wired.

Remember the amygdala? It's still there, in the brains of the people you want to reach, scanning the horizon for physical and verbal threats. Anything that's new needs to be evaluated: even the stuff they will love. Until people can be sure that what you're proposing isn't harmful—or inconvenient or unnecessary—they will remain in resistance.

The first thing to do is get their attention. This is true of everyone— from the people at the office who report to you, to a prospective client, to your family. There are a couple of ways to go about this, so you can move them to listening.

Say Something Interesting or Unusual. Let's say that you're at an industry convention. A portion of the program is devoted to networking. This means you're in a large room with lots of other people. If the thought of this is giving your stomach the jitters, then reread the chapter on getting your brain back!

You are wise, so you've already completed the second "get," which is to get clear on your goals. Here's one I frequently use in these situations: "To have at least three interesting conversations, and meet at least one person I would like to see again."

You can start to create these interesting conversations by having a good elevator pitch. This is something pithy you can say in 20 to 30 seconds (or even less time, if you're really good!) that leaves a memorable, positive impression and encourages the other person to ask, "What does that mean?" or "How do you do that?"

Here's one of my favorites, from speaking consultant Lois Creamer: "I work with professional speakers who want to book more business and make more money." If you're a speaker, chances are good that these are two hot buttons for you—so you'll want to talk with Lois!

Listen First. Most of us wander through life feeling chronically unseen and unheard. A great way to move people from resisting to listening is by listening yourself—and giving them all of your attention.

If we're still at that networking event, you would be the one who asks the other person to speak first. Then you would follow up with "What does that mean?" "How do you do that?" or some other question that encourages the person to tell you more. In general, people welcome the opportunity and will be glad to talk (which might also soothe some of the nerves that *you* have at this event). After a minute or two, to repay your attentiveness, most people will ask what *you* do. Because you have been listening, you now know how to couch your elevator pitch in the way that would be the most interesting to and memorable for *this* person.

Show Your Concern. You will face situations where the conversation is not as genial as this. A good example would be a distraught teenager, such as Fred. My attempts at this were a bit lame: "I like you and thought you liked me." It would have been better had I said, "Fred: I can see that you're mad." Wild understatement, but I have to start *some*place without inflaming the situation! "I want to help. Please tell me what's going on."

When people feel seen and heard, their guard goes down. That means they're much more willing to share what's happening with them. Of course your interest must be genuine. Even when upset, most of us can tell when someone is just feeding us a line for their own purposes.

Listening

Now that you have someone's attention, you have to say something (written or verbal) worthy of keeping it.

Play Back What You Heard. In the last chapter, we talked about your reticular activating system (RAS). Remember that example of being in a crowd and hearing your favorite movie referenced in another conversation? Apply the same idea here.

By listening to the words and thoughts that the people you're trying to reach are using—and then replaying them—you can wake up their RAS and get them to tune in to *you*.

There was a time when I was hired to start the Public Relations Department at a Fortune 1000 services company in Minneapolis. One day, after the chairman read an article in *The Wall Street Journal*, he said to me, "I've decided that we need to have a corporate culture, and our corporate culture will be, 'We are the low-cost producer.'" I felt it was my duty to tell him, "This is more of a slogan than a culture statement. We already *have* a culture. If we want to know what it is, then we need to 1) bring in a consultant that will help us do the research to uncover this, 2) determine what we want the culture to *be*, and then 3) create action steps and communications to help us get there."

You better believe he was disappointed in my response. He just wanted me to say, "Yes, what a wonderful idea!" Now you know why I've only had one corporate job ... But I can promise you, if I had brought a proposal to him on making "We are the low-cost producer" our corporate culture, he would have signed off on it in a flash!

Convey Rather than Convince. This is a great approach when you're dealing with either someone you don't know well or a person you need to move to action. Let's say that you're in a new business presentation with a prospect. Chances are good that this person is waiting for you to "sell" her something—at least that's what her amygdala is telling *her*. You've heard the truism dozens of times: people want to *buy*—they don't want to be *sold*.

44

That's why choosing to convey is so great. You have spent more time listening than speaking in this meeting. You have a sound sense of what this person and her company need. You also know that what you're offering will help her. Here's where most of us make a mistake. We think it's our job to *convince* her to work with us. Not so! In part, because taking that tack can make us feel and look a little desperate—and few things are more unattractive in that moment.

Instead, conveying the reasons why what we can do will help her solve her problem or get what she wants is much more worthwhile for all sides. You are speaking from your place as an expert, with ideas that are tailored to her needs. She doesn't feel like you're a used car salesman, pressuring her into something she doesn't need. Her resistance goes down and she's more likely to listen. Since you know what you're talking about, you can get her to consider what you recommend.

Because—let's face it—once we have to convince someone to do something, we've already lost the battle.

Considering

This is the point where we move people from "yes, but ..." to simply "yes." Here are two techniques that can help you get there.

Show Why Their Objections Really Aren't So. Research indicates that people say "no" to a new idea an average of five times before they say "yes." Their objections usually focus on these four areas:

1. We have no money
2. We don't need this
3. We don't need it *now*
4. We don't trust you

They're usually not blunt or honest enough to say the last one, so they may give you one of the others as a smokescreen. Because you know this, you can take two courses of action that will make you more effective in the considering process.

One: Don't just think of the top *five* objections they could raise on your recommendation—consider the top *10*. Then be ready to show why these really aren't the deal breakers they might think.

One of my personal favorite twists on this comes from sales coach and motivational speaker Brian Tracy. He calls it the "Instant Reverse" approach to closing a sale. When your potential customer says, "I can't afford it," you respond with "That's exactly why you should agree to it!" Then you follow this with some logical reasons why that is true, such as the cost will never be lower than it is now. If the prospect says, "I'm not interested," you counter with "That's exactly why you should do this! Our best customers weren't interested when we first approached them, and now they're very happy. Their skepticism helped them get the most from what we offer." This requires some chutzpah, but it's guaranteed to turn the conversation in a new direction.

Two: Preempt objections by answering them in your conversation, memo/proposal or presentation. Do it in a matter-of-fact way. This reduces the chances that people might get concerned about a problem they hadn't yet thought about until now.

Make It All About Them. I recently spoke about storytelling at a meeting of marketing professionals. One of them, who worked with a consumer packaged goods company, came up to me afterward and said, "How do I get salespeople to *stop* talking about product features? Nothing turns a prospective customer off faster!"

His first point was spot-on. (Although I've seen other horrible sales gaffes quickly turn off prospects.) People in professional services are just as guilty as those selling products. Here are the issues I've seen first-hand.

We want to show that we know. We've spent time learning things about our products and business and wish to share this. Unfortunately, sometimes we're so focused on passing along our knowledge that we're not even looking at the people across from us—and noticing that their eyes are glazing over.

Once I was working with the world's largest investor relations agency—teaching CEOs and CFOs how to talk with their investors. I went on a new business meeting with the head salesman, William, because I would lead the team if this became our account. We were visiting with the management of a family-run company that owned a chain of movie theaters.

William had a set presentation he gave each time (I'd sat through it before). Much of this consisted of sliding sheets of paper across the table at the prospect—focusing on different reasons why our firm was "the best." He also had a tendency to play to the person in the room who nodded in agreement and seemed most receptive. In this case, it was the controller. Unfortunately, the decision-maker was the chairman.

The chairman interrupted William in mid-spiel and asked, "Do you have an office in LA?"

William was flustered. "LA? Los Angeles?" he sputtered.

"No," said the chairman, in a southern Kansas drawl, "Los Alamitos."

"Los Alamitos?" William asked, still lost.

"Laugh, William," I said, "it's a joke." Then I went on to tell the chairman that we were opening an office in Los Angeles in a few months.

This story reminds me that we can get so lost in *what we want to say* that we totally miss *what people need to hear*. They'll generally give us clues—or tell us outright. But if we're stuck in pushing information at them, we'll miss our chance.

We seek comfort, not success. Persuasion in general—and sales in particular—can be anxious territory for us. To minimize our discomfort, it's human nature to go for the familiar. In this instance, that could be talking about good ol' product features or getting into detailed descriptions of what we do. While this may soothe *us*, it doesn't do much for the people we're trying to reach.

This approach also can have the unfortunate effect of talking people *out* of willing to do. They have reached the point where they're ready to move ahead with our idea—and yet we're still talking. And talking some more. They can lose patience with us—as they should, for not paying attention to them—and throw out the idea, with us behind it.

For several years, once a month I would travel the country teaching workshops for a training company. I had three fascinating subjects: finance and accounting for non-financial managers (for people who were afraid of numbers), financial statement analysis (for people who knew something about numbers but didn't know what to do with them once they showed up in financial statements), and business writing and grammar made easy and fun (which most people don't believe is possible).

Early on, I spent a lot of time trying to "do it right." I worried about whether I was presenting good information in an interesting way. I focused on developing the right materials, moving around the room, what I was doing with my hands, if people liked me, etc. No wonder I typically didn't sleep well the night before!

Then I saw a documentary on a middle school in the south, whose eighth grade class project was on the holocaust. The teacher spearheading this effort had never presented on the topic before. In an interview, she mentioned fretting about doing a good job. Then she shared an idea that shifted my entire perspective. It was something to the effect of, "I realized it was not about me—it was about helping my students get something out of this."

What a freeing idea!

I no longer needed to pay attention to what I was doing at a given moment—because *my performance wasn't important.* Making sure that the people who were coming got what they wanted from the experience was the thing. If I were focusing on *them,* then I didn't have time to be nervous about *me.*

The irony, of course, is that suddenly I became a better trainer. I mingled with participants before the workshop and during breaks, asking what they wanted to get from the experience—and if that was happening for them. I devised a system so that I would learn everyone's name by the first break. And people rewarded me by getting more involved and asking more questions during the day—then asking what other courses I taught, so they could take another one with me. I had lightened up, which made it easier for them to learn.

There are plenty of goals, strategies and tactics you can use to become more persuasive. But these will only work if you're willing to do two things:

1. Face the discomfort of stepping away from what you've always done
2. Deal with the disappointment of not getting it right immediately —because you're trying something new and need practice to get better

But ultimately, I promise that you'll be more successful—and feel "lighter" in the process.

Before your next important meeting—with your boss, your client, your board of directors or your spouse—consider where those people are on the Persuasion Cycle. Tailor your communications to meet them where they are. You'll be amazed at how much more effective you become.

- Before you can persuade anyone, you need to know the steps their brains go through to agree with you:
  1. Resisting
  2. Listening
  3. Considering
  4. Willing to do
  5. Doing
  6. Glad they did
  7. Willing to do again

- Applying the Persuasion Cycle to the new business process tells us:
  1. The purpose of a cold call is to have a conversation (move from resisting to listening)
  2. The purpose of a conversation is to get a meeting (from listening to considering)
  3. The purpose of a meeting is to get permission to do a proposal (from considering to willing to do)
  4. The purpose of the proposal is to get the job (from willing to do to doing)

- The beauty of the Persuasion Cycle is that you only need to move people along to the next step—rather than immediately convert them to your point of view.

- The buy-in part of the cycle is resisting/listening/considering. If you can't get people through this, you don't have a chance to persuade them. They'll develop buyer's remorse and make you go through that portion of the process all over again.

- To take people from resisting to listening, say something interesting or unusual, listen first and show your concern.

- To take people from listening to considering, show why their objections aren't so, and make it all about them.

- To successfully persuade others, you have to move out of your comfort zone and try things you haven't done before, and be willing to mess up while you practice.

Practice Persuasion Awareness Exercise

1. Write three events coming up this week during which you'll need to persuade someone to do something. These could be meetings, phone conversations or something you write (memos, emails, etc.).

    a. _____

    b. _____

    c. _____

2. List where that person is/those people are on the Persuasion Cycle.

    a. _____

    b. _____

    c. _____

3. Identify the tactics for moving them along to the next stage.

    a. _____

    _____

    b. _____

    _____

c.

_____

_____

4. Afterward, write what you tried and the results you got.

    a.

    _____

    _____

    b.

    _____

    _____

    c.

    _____

    _____

5. How was this different from just "winging it"?

    a.

    _____

    _____

    b.

    _____

    _____

c.

Get Communicating:
Part One – Get the Message Right

"Good communication is just as stimulating as black
coffee, and just as hard to sleep after."
– Anne Morrow Lindbergh

It feels as though you have millions of things to do today. You can't give everything equal attention. So you select where you're going to spend your mental energy. Too often—when it comes to thinking about what we want to say or write—we choose autopilot.

Some situations come out of the blue, such as mine with Fred. But I was a childcare worker in a group home. If I had been savvier, I could have anticipated that the day would come when I would face a dangerous situation with one of my boys. I could have talked to more experienced people about what might happen—and what I could do. But the thought never crossed my mind.

Fortunately, you're smarter than that. And so am I—*now*.

This chapter focuses on a process you can use to develop the messages you need *before* you need them. Now you're ready to do this, because you have your wits about you (you got your brain back), you know what you want (you got clear goals), and you understand how to meet the people you want to reach where they are (you got them pegged on the Persuasion Cycle).

Where Do You Begin?

When it comes to communicating—and particularly writing—we all have our fears. I call them "brain blocks." Do any of these sound familiar:

- *Belittler's block:* This is the fear that we have nothing to say that would interest others. It quickly degenerates to "and what makes me think they would want to listen?" and on down the lack of confidence rat hole.

- *Babbler's block:* This is the fear that we will say too much and turn off people. They'll think we're either full of ourselves or not very smart.

- *Ballerina's block:* This is the fear that the subject we need to discuss is too sensitive or taboo. We feel the need to pirouette around it to avoid the negative spotlight we would be in by naming it.

All of these things can give us creative constipation—so we stare at a blank screen or sheet of paper and feel paralyzed.

Choose to do this instead. Warm yourself up by using a process followed by journalists, called "The five Ws and an H." Answer these questions:

1. *Who:*
   Who am I writing to/speaking with?
   Where are they on the Persuasion Cycle?
   Where are they in the company hierarchy?
   What is my personal relationship with them?

2. *What:*
   What do these people already know?
   What will they do with this information?

3. *When:*
   When will people see/hear this?
   When will they act?

4. *Where:*

    Where will people see/hear this?

    Where do these people do most of their work?

    Where will they need to go to get approval to act?

5. *Why:*

    Why am I communicating now?

    Why should these people care or respond?

6. *How:*

    How interested are they in my message?

    How will they feel about the information?

Next, take five minutes and use one of these two simple brain block busting tactics to get started. Which one you choose depends upon how you think—literally.

Freewriting

Use this approach if you're more of a right-brained and creative sort.

Grab a blank sheet of paper (lined or unlined—your choice) and a pen. Set a timer for five minutes. Think about your topic and write without stopping. All you want to do is get the ideas out of your head. Use these principles of brainstorming:

1. Don't censor yourself: write everything that occurs to you, no matter how far-fetched it appears.
2. Don't pay attention to grammar, spelling, punctuation, word choice, sentences—anything but your subject.
3. If you find yourself between thoughts, then looking at the "five Ws and an H" questions may spark you.

When the timer goes off, stop writing.

Most of the time, you'll be amazed by the number of messages you can generate in such a short period! Now go back and pick out the good ones.

Mindmapping

This is a better choice if you're more of an analytical, logical thinker.

Again, you need a blank sheet of paper and a pen, and a timer set for five minutes. Not surprisingly, this approach is a little more structured:

1. Pick a phrase that represents the main issue or topic. Write it in the center of the page. Then draw a circle around it.
2. Brainstorm without considering if something is a "good" or a "bad" idea. Write a short phrase that represents each. Then circle it and draw a line back to the main issue/topic in the middle of the page.
3. When the timer sounds, stop.
4. Now you have your best thoughts all on one easy-to-read sheet. You also have a few clinkers, which you wrote down so you could keep your mind and hand in motion.
5. Look at each idea. Think about how important or relevant it is. Then place a number above it that represents this, starting at "1" for the most important. Cross out any that don't fit.
6. Now you have an outline of what you want to share, and the order in which to present it.

Why This Works

In both cases, thinking about *ideas* uses your *left brain*. The physical activity of *writing* (words in freewriting, plus the circles and lines in mindmapping) uses your *right brain*. This means your entire brain is involved in problem solving!

Avoid any predilection you have for doing this on your computer or using the mindmapping software programs out there. In this instance, I believe the low-tech approach of writing by hand better serves you. That's because you need the feel of holding a pen and the arm movement of taking it around a page (or holding a stylus and skittering it across a tablet) to engage your right brain. Sitting at the computer gives you minimal arm movement—just your fingers, really—which emphasizes the mainly left-brained activity of typing out words.

There's also something very freeing and childlike about making big scrawls without worrying how they look as you do them!

The five-minute limit really works. It's enough time to get the most important points out of your head. I've found much of what I come up with after that is repetitious or doesn't add a lot—my time is better spent organizing the good stuff I've already come up with.

Creating Messages That Work

Now that you've loosened yourself up, it's time to get strategic about your communication opportunity. Here's a system I've taught to executives and middle managers across the country. I like it because it gives them clarity and direction. They like it because it works.

I recently used this in training with project managers and construction superintendents at a commercial construction company. Let's use them as an example.

Building a Case for a Construction Company

Here was their issue. They wanted to be more effective in new business meetings with potential customers. The process for getting a new client was very structured and repeatable. The construction firm would respond to a request for proposal. When it made the initial cut—most often because it was close to the price target the customer was seeking—this would be followed by an in-person interview. In addition to the user (the tenant, or the company that needed something built or built-out in an existing building) other related parties could be there.

Since price was not much of a differentiating factor at this point, the company needed to do something to set itself apart from its competition. The owners decided one of the best ways to do this would be to have the client meet the members of the team they would be working with.

While a good strategy, the initial results were disappointing. Project managers and construction superintendents knew how to *do* their jobs, but not how to *talk* about these in a meeting. This meant they often said little—besides their names and job titles—or got nervous and said too much. The latter could be a problem if the interview process only lasted 15 or 30 minutes.

The goal for our work together was to help these two groups 1) know what to say when they went into a meeting, and 2) feel comfortable about sharing the information.

This is how we did it—by asking the people being trained to answer a series of questions. For the purposes of this exercise, we defined the job as building a customized office space for a client on the 24th floor of a commercial building in downtown Chicago. Here are the questions—and how they answered these.

Step #1: Who are the different audiences involved?

They brainstormed the types of people who would attend the interview. These included the architect (who is designing the space or building), the owner's representative (paying attention to the interests of the company that owns the building), the building engineer (knowing what worked within this particular facility), and the user (who would use the space that is being designed).

Step #2: What does each audience think of you (if they know you) and your company? Do they like and trust you? Do they see you as different from your competitors?

The idea is to know if there are any plusses that we can capitalize on (they know our work and trust us) or minuses we must overcome (they have no connection with us yet, or we did a project in times past that did not go well) going in to the meeting. Here's how they responded.

1. *Architect:* This woman knows us, has worked with us before and been happy with the results. She was the one who suggested we bid this job.
2. *Owner's representative:* He has heard of our firm but never worked with us. He has a neutral opinion about us.
3. *Building engineer:* He knows other building engineers who have worked with us but also is neutral.
4. *User:* He has seen our signs on other jobs but knows nothing about us.

Step #3: Put yourself in each audience's place. What do they really want to know about working with your company?

Many times we can get so caught up in what *we* want to say that we don't even consider what people want to hear. (Remember Los Alamitos?) It's useful to spend a few minutes seeing things from their perspective. And it's always a plus when more than one audience wants to know the same thing.

These are the ideas they shared.

1. **Architect:**
   - How you will build my design
   - How you will be on time
   - How you will be on budget
2. **Owner's representative:**
   - How you will solve my problems
3. **Building engineer:**
   - How you will preserve my building
   - How much mechanical systems knowledge you have about my building
4. **User:**
   - Why you are the best company for this job
   - How you are trustworthy
   - How you will stay within the budget

- How you will live within the schedule

Step #4: Bring the focus back to you. What do you really want each person to know about what the company offers?

While you want to make sure each audience's communications needs are met, that doesn't mean you do this at your expense. You have goals for this meeting and there are ideas you need to share to reach them. That was true for these project managers and construction superintendents.

1. *Architect:*
   - We will make you look good
   - We won't throw you under the bus by complaining about your designs to other parties
   - We will respect your designs and love them almost as much as you do
   - We will propose solutions for building your designs rather than complain about problems
2. *Owner's representative:*
   - We will be in constant communication with you
   - We will make certain everyone works together as a team (our people and the subcontractors) with the goal of doing a great job
   - We will deliver on our promises
3. *Building engineer:*
   - We will respect and rely on your knowledge of the building
   - We will keep the building safe for your tenants, staff and visitors
   - We will have a "low impact" on the building and the people who use it
4. *User:*
   - Our customer service extends beyond completing the job, and we will return to handle other changes and upgrades you need

Step #5: Review the last two steps. What are the common ideas: the messages each audience needs to hear and you want to share? (If there isn't any common ground, discuss why this is so and what to do about it.)

As you have already seen, our construction company people were able to identify a number of overlapping ideas:

1. Delivering the job on-time and on-budget
2. Maintaining the integrity of the space
3. Regular communication
4. Team player
5. Trust goes both ways

It's rare that there is no intersection between what people want to hear and what you wish to tell them. When this *does* happen, it's time to investigate your motives for communicating. Is this a difficult conversation where you'd rather not tell someone what he wants to hear? Are her wishes so different from yours that your goal is to change her mind? Communication is tough when there is little to no common ground. Many times it's up to you to find it—or to create it first.

Step #6: What are the three most important messages? What are the proof points or supporting strategies needed for each?

Three is a magic number for me. It's easy to remember three messages for a meeting, a call, a question and answer session, or a written communication. It's also easy for your audience to recall. This forces you to focus on the most important ideas.

In addition, having three supporting points for each of your messages shows the people you want to reach that you have thought through your position and have come prepared. Since your goal is to persuade them, you can use these sub-points to preempt some of their objections in advance.

After looking at the "common ground" messages in the last step, our construction group prioritized them into the top three and developed these supporting ideas for each:

1. <u>We will do the project on time and on budget</u>
    a. We will recognize items that have a long lead time and get these in place so the construction process isn't interrupted
    b. We will prequalify our subcontractors, so they are ready to work at the times when they are needed
    c. We will look for potential issues, recognize them early, and take action before they become problems
2. <u>We will make communication a priority</u>
    a. We will be in constant contact, letting you know about any issues that are coming up
    b. We will send daily progress reports so you always know what's happening
    c. We will tailor our communications to the needs of each team member—knowing that the building engineer and the user, for example, are interested in different things
3. <u>We are team players</u>
    a. We have great respect for what each team member—architect, owner's representative, building engineer and user—contributes to the process
    b. We won't blindside anyone at meetings
    c. We will make sure there are clear roles for all team members and that everyone understands these

Step #7: Create a "mini-speech." What are two to three sentences you can use to summarize the situation and your main ideas?

You can see how the message development process creates two things: 1) clarity for our construction company people on what they need to say, and 2) messages that work for everyone who comes to the interview table. But this is the point when things often begin to get mucked up.

In the weeks following the session during which we developed the messages, we brought in teams of two men for follow-up training: a project manager paired with a construction supervisor. Because they had two basic roles in the interview meeting—to introduce themselves and to answer questions—we wanted to help them practice these. They also needed to see how they looked and sounded while doing this, so we videotaped them.

These were smart, skilled men. However, most of them already forgot the messages we agreed to and went back to winging it. When asked to introduce themselves, they ranged from just giving their names and their titles, to a ramble about other unrelated jobs they had done. And when asked questions, they focused on what they thought was the literal meaning of the question, rather than what we knew people needed to hear and what our guys wanted to say.

This is why the mini-speech is important. It reminds you of the three messages you really want to give and packages them succinctly. It can be used to open and close a presentation or meeting, or worked into the answer to nearly any question that comes up. (We'll get into Q&A in the next chapter.)

Each man was able to develop a mini-speech that worked best for him, using words that felt comfortable. This also increased the chances that he would use it—and not feel as though he was "spouting the company line."

This training on message development and practice produced a number of tangible results:

1. The construction company gives a consistent message about itself at all interviews.
2. The message it presents focuses on the people it wants to work with—but still includes the ideas it wishes them to understand.
3. The men presenting the messages know what to say and feel more comfortable attending these meetings.
4. The strategy of introducing prospects to their team at an interview—and showcasing the skills these people have—is allowing the company to differentiate itself in the market.
5. Their new business success rate has increased.

Too many times we think of messages as an "either/or" prospect: either we say what *others* want or we talk about what *we* want. From now on, use this process to create a "both/and" situation: the people you're trying to reach get their needs met *and* you don't have to ignore what you want to say to make that happen.

- When we're stumped on what we want to say, this often comes from belittling ourselves, our concern about looking self-centered, or our fear of dealing with sensitive situations or topics.

- Asking ourselves the "Five Ws and an H"— who, what, when, where, why and how—a can give us a better sense of the people we need to reach.

- Taking five minutes to use freewriting (for right-brained people) and mindmapping (for left-brained people) is a good way to do a "brain dump" on a topic. Then we can review all of our good ideas and focus on the ones that are the best fit.

- Use a seven-step process to create messages that not only work for the people you're trying to reach, but you too:
  1. Identify your audiences.
  2. Ask what each audience thinks of you (if they know you) and your company. Do they like and trust you? Do they see you as different from your competitors?
  3. Put yourself in each audience's place. Make a list of what they really want to know about working with you or your company.
  4. Bring the focus back to you. Make a list of what you really want each person to know about what you or the company offers.
  5. Review the last two steps and list the common ideas—the messages each audience needs to hear and you want to share. (If there isn't any common ground, discuss why this is so and what to do about it.)
  6. Narrow your messages down to three. Develop proof points or supporting strategies as needed for each.
  7. Create a "mini-speech": two to three sentences you can use to summarize the situation and your main ideas.

Get In Touch with Your Audience Exercise

1. Think about a report or proposal you will be presenting in the next month. What is it?

_____

2. Analyze the people who will be listening to you by using the Five Ws and an H:

   a. Who

   _____

   _____

   b. What

   _____

   _____

   c. Where

   _____

   _____

d. Why

_____

_____

e. When

_____

_____

f. How

_____

_____

Freewriting and Mindmapping Exercise

1. Get a blank sheet of paper.
2. Set a timer for five minutes.
3. Try freewriting for one project and mindmapping for another. Write without stopping on your topic. See which one best suits you.

Seven Steps for Developing Messages Exercise

Pick a communication event—a presentation, proposal or report—and use these steps to get clear on what you want to say:

1. Identify your audiences.

   a. _____

   b. _____

   c. _____

   d. _____

2. What does each audience think of me? Of the company? Do they like and trust me? Do they see us as different from our competitors?

   a. _____

   b. _____

   c. _____

   d. _____

3. What do they really want to know about this subject?

   a. _____

   b. _____

c. _____

d. _____

4. What do I really want to tell them?

   a. _____

   b. _____

   c. _____

   d. _____

5. What are the common ideas between #3 and #4?

   _____

   _____

   _____

6. What are the top three messages from #5? What proof points or strategies can I share to support them?

   1. _____

      a. _____

      b. _____

      c. _____

2. _____

    a. _____

    b. _____

    c. _____

3. _____

    a. _____

    b. _____

    c. _____

7. What is my "mini-speech": two to three sentences I use to summarize the situation and my main ideas?

_____

_____

_____

_____

Get Communicating:
Part Two – Answer Well

"The single biggest problem in communication is the
illusion that it has taken place."
– George Bernard Shaw

People generally respond to the questions they've been asked. Have you ever sat or stood there, hoping someone will ask the "right" questions that give you the chance to share your main points? Beyond that, many times we're just hoping to *survive* the situation!

Fred never asked me any questions. If I had been wiser, I would have asked *him* one: "What do you want, Fred?" In retrospect, it was clear that he didn't want to hurt me. Otherwise he wouldn't have given me the warning that he would if I tried to call for help. Or he just would have gone ahead and stabbed me.

Although he didn't ask a question outright, what I didn't understand at the time is that one was implied: "Why do I have to do what you're telling me to?" And frankly, even if he'd been able to ask me, I probably would have given him some lame answer. "Because that's my job." "Because those are the rules that all of us have to follow." "Because I'm in charge and I said so." If I were Fred, at this point I'd be tempted to stab me, too!

Here's what we forget. It's just as legitimate for *us* to have a reason to participate in a Q&A session as it is for the people asking the questions. (Remember Get #2: Get Clear on Your Goals?) While you don't want to dodge questions, there are techniques you can use that ensure you get to share your key messages.

Ask Yourself Before They Ask You

What frightens most of us is the idea that someone will ask a question we're not prepared for, making us appear uninformed, incompetent, or just plain stupid. Avoid this by creating a list of questions you're likely to get from each audience and practice your answers.

This is another place where you should never make the mistake of "winging it." That can lead to saying something you don't intend or failing to share your key messages.

By following the process in the last chapter, you already identified what each audience wants. Now develop these three types of questions for each group:

- *Questions you **expect** to be asked.* You anticipate them because you've been in this situation before and heard those questions then, or these would be logical questions to ask under the circumstances. Here were a few for the construction company in the last chapter:

  1. Are you using our preferred subcontractors?
  2. How much supervision will you have on our project?
  3. Have you walked around the space and the building?

- *Questions you **hope** to be asked.* There may be some overlap between these questions and the ones you expect to be asked. In a few minutes, it will be clear why you're doing these, too. Let's go back to our construction company for examples:

  1. Why should we work with your company?
  2. Have you done this type of work before?
  3. When can you start?

- *The most difficult questions you can think of.* These are the questions you don't want to hear. Because getting what you want requires being prepared even in tough situations, you'll think about these in advance. Our construction professionals identified these:

1. What flaws have you found in my architectural drawings?
2. What other projects do you have underway that could pull your attention away from ours?
3. Why is your estimate so much higher than the other competitors' are?

It's OK not to know the answer to every question. If you encounter this situation, explain that you don't have this information and either will find it, or will put the person in touch with someone who knows. Then follow up.

Leading an Effective Q&A

You understand your subject—otherwise people wouldn't be interested in hearing what you have to say. This is called the 90% rule: if you know more about a topic than 90% of the people in the room, then you're an expert! Questions can't hurt you. Poor answers can.

People generally consider the Q&A one of the most critical parts of a meeting. They may prod for hot buttons to see how you stand up under pressure. By understanding how to lead the Q&A as though it's a *conversation*, you stand to make three important gains:

1. Present a positive, credible view of yourself and/or your company
2. Share key messages that inform your audiences (this is your mini-speech)
3. Influence their decision-making process—so you can get what you want

In conversations or meetings with you, clients, executives and employees (and others) use three methods to get information:

- *Direct questions* that tell you specifically what they want to know. Using our construction company, an example of this would be, "How long will it take to do the build-out of the floor in our facility?"

- *Closed-ended questions* are structured for a "yes" or "no" response. "Will you be able to complete the build-out by June?"

- *Open-ended questions or requests* invite you to offer more of what you think is important. "Why do you think your company is the right partner for us on this project?"

People *remember what you said*, not the question. Here are some techniques to help you make the most of *any* question.

Bridging

Bridging is the art of **answering an easy, tough or off-target question and smoothly segueing into one of your messages**. The secret to a successful bridge is to start by giving a short, honest answer to the question. Then you can either 1) ask another question and then answer with one of your important points, or 2) move directly to an idea you want to share. If you can't logically move to one of your messages, then give the short answer and stop.

Bridging allows you to maintain a two-party dialog without giving up control. Let's make your options clear by using some shorthand:

1. *Q (in italics)* = a question from someone else
2. **A** = your answer
3. **a** = your short answer, or "yes" or "no"
4. **Q** = a question you ask yourself

Q A Q A – When you're asked a positive "friendly" question, answer it. Then *ask yourself* a second, related question and answer this. For example:

Q: Why I should we work with your company?

A: We have a record of completing jobs just like this one on time and on budget.

Q: I'm betting everyone you sit across the table from says the same thing, so you're wondering what makes us different.

A: We analyze your project up front to identify items with long lead times, so we make sure those are ordered and arrive when we need them. We also prequalify all of the subcontractors for your project. That means everyone knows what we need from them and when. And we recognize potential issues early and act on them so they don't become problems. For example, on a similar project …

Q a Q A – You also have to answer tough, leading or threatening questions. Keep it short—a word or a sentence. Then translate the question into one that is positive or neutral, and answer this.

Q: Why is your estimate so much higher than the other competitors' are?

a: Not having seen their estimates, I can't really say.

Q: If I were you, I'd be wondering if everything that *should* be included is in *all* of the estimates you're seeing.

A: Since we've done projects like this before, we included something in our base budget that others often treat as an add-on during the job, which increases the total cost later. That is …

Q A A – Answer the positive, easy question, and then add more information from one of your key messages.

Q: How will we know what's going on with the project?

A: We send daily reports to everyone on the team, so you'll always know what's happening.

A: Because we know that each of you looks at this project from a different angle, we don't send the same report to everyone. We take the time to tailor the one you receive to meet your needs. As an owner's representative, for example, the first page of your report will cover ...

Here are some useful examples of bridge language:

- ***Don't know/what I do know ...***
  "I don't know the answer to that question. What I *do* know is ..."

- ***Time***
  "Historically that was the case. Here's what we're doing now ..."

- ***Interpreting the question***
  "It sounds as though what you're really asking is ..."
  "Yes. You also may be wondering ..."
  "If you're asking me ..."
  "As a developer, you also may be interested in knowing our track record on ..."

- ***Importance***
  "That used to be important. What's important *now* is ..."
  "No. Let me explain ..."
  "Yes, and in addition ..."
  "Yes. A more critical question would be ..."

Bridging gets a bad reputation from those who abuse it. Politicians are famous for this. They are renowned for hearing a question and then saying whatever they want: not even bothering to address what was asked. As you can see, that's not bridging—it's obfuscation.

When you bridge, you answer the question first, and then you add something of value that also would be interesting to them. This is because the key messages you developed were created with their needs in mind. Any time you track back to one of these, you're sharing something that your audience wants or needs to know.

Listing

Q 1 2 3 –This technique *allows you to force your questioner to take in more information than he or she expected*. Once you say you have three important points to make, most people will let you do this uninterrupted. Be sure to number each point. Only do this when you have questions that need a lengthy answer.

Q: Have you done this type of work before?
A: Yes. We recently finished a similar project in the Willis Tower. In the process, we used three strategies to help our client that most construction firms don't think of. First, … Second, … Third, … That's why we're sure we can bring your project in on time and on budget.

In general, a three-point answer is ideal. That's the amount of information most people can hold in their short-term memory. Once you get past four points, you've probably lost them somewhere.

Flagging

Q*!*A – This allows you to use language and your voice to *let the questioner know you're about to say something they should know*. Use flagging to answer one of your most important questions or to indicate what you're about to share includes the key idea you'll be discussing.

Q: What other projects do you have underway that could pull your attention away from ours?

! If you remember nothing else about what we've said today, remember this.

A: Your construction superintendent will be at your job site every morning at 9:00, ensuring that your team is in place and understands what needs to be done that day. He also will ... You have our commitment to this process no matter how many other projects we have going on.

Here are other examples of flagging language:

1. "The most important point to remember is ..."
2. "The most exciting thing about working with you on this project is ..."
3. "The real issue is ..."
4. "The real question to ask is ..."

Hooking

Q A ... – This probably is not what you were thinking ... Hooking is the art of *giving a little* **taste** *of an idea, and encouraging the kind of follow-up questions you want*.

Q: Why is your estimate so much higher than your competitors' are?
A: You'd be surprised at the kinds of items our competitors routinely leave out of their estimates ...
Q: Like what?

Here are some other examples of hooking language:

1. "You may be interested in what our other clients say about that ..."
2. "We've got some other exciting new services that will be available soon ..."

3. "We've learned a lot from our experiences with cost-effective build-outs ..."

Hooking is my least favorite Q&A technique for two reasons. First, I understand its purpose is to draw in your questioner and get that person more engaged—because he or she is asking at least one follow-up question. However, it can come off as manipulative or even smarmy.

Second, it relies on the other person to be paying enough attention to ask the next question. To me, this is giving up control of the Q&A session. And, let's face it, the last thing you want to do is sit there, verbally wiggling your eyebrows and winking at the questioner and not have him or her take the bait. The other three approaches are so much more effective and easier to use that I say, "Why risk trying this one and having it backfire?"

Other Q&A Techniques for Use in Meetings or on Calls

When presenting before a large group, use these techniques as a courtesy to your audience and to lead the session—rather than feeling led by it.

- *It's a discussion, not an interrogation* – Once again, think of this as a conversation—if possible, with a friend. If it's a formal session, move away from the podium. In an office, sit across from or next to clients or employees.

- *Ask good questions* – Sometimes you open a Q&A and it takes a while for the first questioner to speak. Everyone can feel uncomfortable during this silence. Rather than hope someone will get up the nerve, *ask yourself a question* that will lead to one of your main messages:

  "If I were you, I'd be wondering about ..."
  "A question I'm frequently asked is ..."

But make sure the question has substance (is on the list of what your audience wants to know) so it doesn't appear as though you're lobbing yourself an easy one.

- *Repeat the question* – If you need to, rephrase it. Whether or not the presentation is being webcast, this is a good way to ensure others heard the question. It also gives you a moment to consider your answer and take the time you need to give a thoughtful reply.

- *If you're speaking to an outside audience, use the first question to explain the company's story* – This group may not have a good sense of what you and your company are all about. If you're not asked to describe your business, find a way to bridge from answering the question to explaining the company. "I think it will help if I explain a bit more about what we do ..."

- *Reinforce good questions and questioners* – "That's a good question ..." (when it is) grabs the interest of listeners (who now want to know the answer) and makes the person who asked it feel insightful. Do this in particular with difficult questions. Don't do it with too many questions, or else it loses its value.

- *Don't repeat negative language from a question in your answer* – This is the prototypical "Are you still beating your wife?" ("My wife Sharon and I are happily married and about to celebrate our 20th wedding anniversary!" Not "I never beat my wife!") If there is a factual error, begin by correcting it—then bridge to one of your messages.

- *If a question at a group meeting or on a call is off topic or requires a lengthy answer, take it offline* – Volunteer to discuss it with the person later, and then move on. Afterward, follow up.

- ***It's OK not to know the answer to every question*** – Once again, if you encounter this situation, don't make a guess, a conjecture or a forecast. Explain that you don't have the information and will either find it or put the person in touch with someone who knows. Then follow through. If it's not an appropriate question—or one you don't intend to answer (for competitive reasons, for example)—say so.

- ***Avoid negative comments or speculation on competitors*** – The first puts you and your company above the fray, and the second avoids the trap of guessing what is happening at another firm. The message you wish to convey is that there are good businesses in your industry, and you'll be happy to explain why you believe yours is among the best.

- ***Use "inviting" body language*** – Begin with a deep breath and a smile. This helps you appear to be friendly, confident, relaxed and in command. Be mindful of your facial expressions, arm and hand movements, and how much you walk around or shift weight from one foot to the other. Avoid the "clenched" look. (We'll delve more into body language—and how to use it to create rapport—in the next chapter, about getting to know your audience.)

- ***Get excited*** – It's rare that a businessperson lets his passion about his company shine through in presentations. Those who are too laid back and appear to be passive diminish their credibility—as well as the interest of their listeners. Being able to "*feel* what you say" helps you connect with your audience (which *wants* you to be excited about your subject). This also means that you'll use shorter sentences, crisper language, and more inflection in your voice—qualities that make it easier to listen to and agree with you.

- Don't be a victim in Q&A, waiting around for someone to ask the questions you *want* to answer. You have as much reason to share your thoughts as they do to get their questions addressed!

- Prepare yourself by developing three types of questions beforehand: 1) those you *expect* to be asked, 2) those you *want* to be asked, and 3) the hard questions you hope you *won't* be asked.

- Treat the Q&A as though it's a conversation rather than an interrogation. When someone tries to put you on the spot, remember this. You know more about this subject than 90% of the people in the room, so you are the expert.

- People will ask you one of three types of questions: 1) direct questions (looking for the information they want), 2) closed-ended questions (looking for a yes or no answer), or 3) open-ended questions (looking for you to share what's important).

- People remember what you said, not the question.

- *Bridging* allows you to answer the question people ask and then "bridge" to one or more of the key points you want to share.

- *Listing* gives you the chance to provide your listeners with detailed information and hold the floor the entire time you do this. That happens because you let them know there are several parts to the answer.

- *Flagging* helps you get their attention by informing them you're about to share something important—so listen up.

- *Hooking* teases people with a partial answer and then invites them to ask a follow-up question to learn more. Be careful about this one. It can come off as manipulative. It also gives up control of the Q&A as you wait for them to ask the next logical question—and they might not!

- There are many techniques you can use to help everyone (including you) get more from the Q&A. These range from asking yourself the first question (to break the ice) to repeating the question so everyone can hear it (and take out any negative wording), to getting excited about your subject (because people want to be around others who are passionate).

What to Do Now

Prep Your Questions Exercise

1. What was the report or proposal for which you developed messages at the end of the last chapter?

    _____

2. Think of three *questions you expect people will ask.*

    a. _____

    b. _____

    c. _____

3. What are three *questions you hope you'll be asked?*

    a. _____

    b. _____

    c. _____

4. Come up with three *difficult questions you wish no one will ask.*

    a. _____

    b. _____

    c. _____

Prep Your Answers Exercise

1. Choose one of the questions you expect people will ask (#2 on the prior page). Answer it here using ***bridging***.

    _____

    _____

    _____

    _____

2. Pick one of the questions from #3. Use ***listing*** to answer it.

    _____

    _____

    _____

    _____

3. Select one of the questions from #4. Address it with ***flagging***.

    _____

    _____

    _____

    _____

4. Take any question from the last exercise and answer it with *hooking*.

_____

_____

_____

_____

Bonus Answer Exercise

Pick any question from the first exercise. Now answer the same question using *each* of your four Q&A techniques.

1. Write your question.

_____

_____

2. Answer it with *bridging*.

_____

_____

_____

_____

3. Answer it with *listing*.

_____

_____

_____

_____

4. Answer it with *flagging*.

_____

_____

_____

_____

5. Answer it with *hooking*.

_____

_____

_____

_____

6. Evaluate your answers. Which technique felt as though it was the best one to use for this question? Why?

Get Communicating:
Part Three – Know Your Audience

"The fault, dear Brutus, is not in our stars,
but in ourselves ..."
– William Shakespeare

We consider ourselves relatively self-aware people. We think about what we want to say before we say it. Sometimes we even practice our messages before a big meeting or conversation. And often, when something doesn't come off well, we blame others. We soothe ourselves by saying, "I did everything I could. They were too blind to see what a good idea this is."

When I have those moments, I think of this pie chart. It frightens me every time I see it.

How We Get Information from Other People

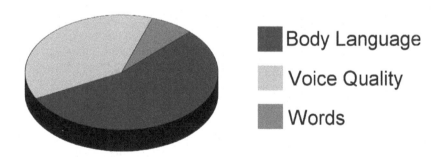

Ninety-three percent of the information we get about a person comes from nonverbal communication. This is divided between voice tone and quality (38%) and body language (a whopping 55%). That means words only contribute about 7% to our impressions. I've spent a good deal of my career helping people get clear on what they need to say—the way we just worked through our messages and handling Q&A—so of course this idea unnerves me. But I can't dispute its truth.

There was nothing more powerful than Fred's body language—standing three feet from me and holding that machete as though he were ready to chop me with it. And that growl in his voice when he threatened to cut me. It really didn't matter *what* he was saying!

Here's the good news. You can use the nonverbal—as well as written and spoken—information people are sending to learn how they think. And then you can add this to your toolkit as part of getting them to do what you want.

Read Their Bodies to Read Their Minds

There are times when you and the people you're trying to persuade will agree on goals and strategies and other times when your opinions will differ. You always want to ensure that the information you provide to them, and the way you give it, increases the chances that they will *get* it. One way to accomplish this is by acknowledging—and working with—their learning and communication styles.

Learning Styles

According to Neil Fleming's VAK (Visual, Auditory, Kinesthetic) Model, there are three primary ways in which people learn.

The "Looker"
These people think mainly in pictures and images. This is the most prevalent style: about 75% of people are Lookers. You can identify them by watching for these signs:

1. They have good posture and their shoulders are tense.
2. They often have thin lips.
3. They frequently have wrinkles on their foreheads. This happens because people generally look up, raise their eyebrows, furrow their brows and breathe faster when they remember something they have *seen*.
4. They look in your eyes while speaking and listening.
5. They choose clothes and decorate their offices and homes for visual impact.

Here is how you build rapport with a Looker:

1. Speak in images whenever possible, since this is how they like to get information:

   "I see what you mean."

   "What's your view on this?"

   "Here's what his comments reveal to me."

   "Show me."

   "Take a look at this."
2. Look in their eyes as much as possible when listening or speaking. These people literally believe that if you aren't looking at their faces, you aren't seeing or paying attention to them. This lets them know they are important to you, and that you are interested in them.
3. If you are *not* a Looker, don't be unnerved by the amount of eye contact these people give you. They are not trying to be confrontational—this is just how they get information.

The "Listener"

These people think mainly in sounds: words and noises. About 20% of people are Listeners. They share these characteristics:

1. Their shoulders usually are slightly rounded.
2. They frequently hold their heads slightly down and to the side. This happens because people look to their left side, tilt their heads a bit and breathe evenly when they remember something they have *heard*. In addition, it naturally points one of their ears in your direction so they can better hear you.
3. They often put a hand up to their face or ear, called the "telephone posture."
4. Their lips may move when they are thinking through something, or they may mumble or speak out loud. This is because they are literally talking to themselves when processing information.
5. They most often look away from others when speaking or listening.
6. They frequently "drum" with their fingers and have music on in the background.

Keep these things in mind when communicating with a Listener:

1. Emphasize sounds in your descriptions:
   "I want to hear what you think."
   "That sounds good to me."
   "What does that tell you?"
   "Let's talk about that."
   "I'd like to speak with you."
2. Don't give them too much eye contact: this makes them feel uncomfortable. Look away then back to them when you speak and listen.
3. If you are *not* a Listener, don't feel ignored when you are not receiving much eye contact. These people still are paying attention to what you are saying—unless they're wearing ear plugs!

The "Toucher"

This group processes information through emotions and physical activity. They make up about 5% of the population. In addition to being more likely to touch people than the other two groups, here are ways you can identify them:

1. They tend to lean toward you in a conversation.
2. They frequently look down to their right, round their shoulders and breathe deeply—because this is what people do when remembering something they have *felt*.
3. They generally have full lips and deep voices.
4. Their movements are loose and relaxed.
5. They choose their clothes and design their surroundings based on comfort rather than style.

When conversing with a "Toucher," use these techniques:

1. Emphasize feelings or tactile words in your conversation.
   "How do you feel about that?"
   "Let's get in touch."
   "I'm having trouble grasping this."
   "I'm going to make contact with him."
   "How would you like me to get hold of you?"
2. Feel free to touch them when you want to emphasize a point.
3. If you are *not* a Toucher, don't feel your space is being invaded if they lean in or touch you. And do your best not to stiffen up if they make physical contact.

Which style are you? Of course your brain is flexible, so you can think in more than one way. But you *will* have a dominant approach. Close your eyes, take a deep breath and remember an important event in your life. How does it come back to you? Do you "see" it—in colors and shapes and pictures? Do you describe it in words? Do you remember how you felt—

or how different objects felt in your hands? These are the important clues that tell you how you think.

Learning the Hard Way

Before understanding the connection between body language and how people think, I made a number of gaffes. Here is the most spectacular.

One of my clients was the controller at a company. We had been in one-on-one meetings across a conference table on many occasions. He never looked me in the eye: he seemed to be looking at the table in front of me. At first I thought it was that he just liked to focus on "the numbers." My next guess was that he was socially inept. Then I developed the sneaking suspicion that he was looking at my chest, which offended me. The day came when I decided to do something about this.

At our next meeting, I leaned down toward the table—to put my face in his line of vision. "Excuse me," I said. "I'm up here!" and sat up straight.

Thinking of this still makes me cringe today!

The man was a Listener. The constant eye contact I was giving him made him nervous, making it even less likely that he would look at my face. And, of course, no stunt on my part was going to change that he processed information through words and sounds, so looked down and to the side while doing this. It's a wonder he didn't fire me! After all, an essential part of getting people to do what you want is not annoying them.

With the information I have today, I would treat this man much better. This would involve looking at him briefly and then looking away as either one of us speaks. It would mean pointing one -of my ears in his direction most of the time. I also would use more language with sound components in it.

The irony is that I am a Listener, too. I remember movie lines, song lyrics and grammar rules. Because the communication industry, where I have spent much of my career, is filled with Lookers—and they are the biggest part of the population—I learned to take on those physical characteristics and values. I can also summon images of places I've been, but that's still not my primary mode of thought. As you're about to see, I have particularly strong "mirror neurons."

Your Brain is Here to Help

It's true: giving Lookers more eye contact, giving Listeners less, and reaching for the hand of a Toucher in conversation helps to create rapport. Fortunately, your subconscious mind is also on the case.

We all have something called mirror neurons. They were discovered in studies of monkeys in the 1990s. The upshot is that when the monkeys observed a student eating an ice cream cone, the same neurons fired in the monkeys' brains as if *they* were also eating something!

Mirror neurons are particularly focused on reading facial expressions. Some researchers even postulate that the mirror neurons in those with autism or schizophrenia don't function well, which is why they have trouble associating meaning with what they see on people's faces. Other experts believe that mirror neurons not only mimic movement and facial expressions but *understand* what they mean.

Here is the important idea for us as persuasive communicators. When we're sitting across from someone, and we see her cradle her chin in her right hand, our brain reacts as though we're doing the same thing. And a lot of times, that's just what we'll do. In a way, our brains are suggesting our bodies copy the behavior of the person we're watching. In the jungle days, this probably was a great survival technique—helping you fit in with the crowd. Now that you know this, you'll notice that you're folding your arms the way the person you're in conversation with is doing—or vice versa.

Actively mirroring the physical actions of the person you want to connect with *does* help build rapport. Remember: 55% of the information you get from someone comes from body language. When the person you want to reach leans in—and you lean in, too—their subconscious mind registers this as simpatico. You help them feel more comfortable physically, and their brains pick this up as agreeing with them. And you don't even have to think about it. Your brain is automatically helping you to be more persuasive!

Build on this by being aware of the body language of the people you want to reach and mirroring it. Then watch how much faster they are at ease with you.

Knowing Communication Styles

Just as there are three ways that people think and learn, there are four primary ways in which people communicate.

- **The "Doer":** This person is action- and results-oriented, competitive, decisive and often a workaholic. His communication style is to quickly get to the point. In doing this, he often can be abrupt.

- **The "Thinker":** This person is conservative, analytical, detail-oriented and slow to decide. She wants to consider all of the information before taking action. Her communication style is wordy—in service of wishing to explain the entire picture.

- **The "Feeler":** This is a people-oriented person who is concerned with relationships. His communication style is to be persuasive, enthusiastic and creative.

- **The "Creator":** This person is scholarly, thinks abstractly and in concepts. Her communication style is to be creative and take longer to get to the point.

Which of these styles is yours? Most people don't bother to ask. They go blithely through their day using *their* approach on *everyone*. Not surprisingly, they can end up shooting themselves in the foot—because they're not paying attention to how other people like to *get* information.

Applying Styles Persuasively

I had a coworker who was a Creator. He reveled in data and was fascinated by minutia. As a financial analyst, he had chosen his career well. He loved developing voluminous reports that explained why and when certain investors would buy a company's stock.

Our client, who was the CEO of a public company, was a Doer. He had neither the time nor the inclination to wade through 20 pages of text to learn the answer to his question. He also had little patience for meetings during which the financial analyst got into the weeds on describing past and future shareholders. At one point he turned to me—when my coworker had left the room—and said, "This guy is the difference between taking a local versus an express train!"

My role became clear. Every time the financial analyst wrote a memo, I edited it. This included reducing the size in general by removing redundant and wordy sentences. It also meant adding subheads to make important points, indicate what was being covered where, and visually break up pages of text.

Then I created a one-page executive summary—with short paragraphs or bullet points that telegraphed the main ideas. The CEO quickly got what he needed and could refer to the longer document if he wanted more details on something.

When we met with the CEO, I became the facilitator. I interviewed my coworker in advance to get a good handle on what he knew—and what we needed to share with the CEO. I presented the information—so we wouldn't get lost on a tangent up front. Then the financial analyst answered the CEO's questions. I watched the CEO's body language (he was a Looker), noticing when he was becoming impatient—by glancing around the room rather than at my coworker. That's the time when I would jump in and move us along.

Using this tag-team approach allowed us to satisfy *our* needs by the satisfying the *CEO's*. He said "yes" to our ideas more often because we were presenting them in a way that appealed to him.

Now that you know *your* style, think about the communication styles of the people you need to persuade. If these are different, what can you do to modify your approach so it appeals to them?

Questioner Styles

As long as we're on the subject of meetings, you'll notice people use different techniques to gather information—and determine what you're willing and unwilling to give. Some may be using this as an opportunity to make themselves look good—or you look bad. Some are genuinely interested in what you have to say, but they are just inept at asking questions.

Always start with the assumption of good will—that people are asking because they want to know something—until you have proof otherwise. Here's how you can deal with difficult questioners and still get your messages heard.

Omniscient Authority

Problem: She expects you to know everything. Sometimes she likes to rub it in when she discovers a question you can't answer. You have the sneaking suspicion she uses this as a way to feel superior to you—or demonstrate this to others in the room.

Solution: We often can have two defensive knee-jerk reactions to this. First, we can make up something—because we don't want to give her the satisfaction of finding the edge of our knowledge. Second, we can tell her the question is off target and try to make her feel some discomfort for asking it. The best approach is to be honest and direct: "That's not my area of expertise, but I'll try to find the information for you." Then keep your word and follow up.

The Machine Gun

Problem: He fires multi-part questions at you, never giving you time to respond. Ultimately you may feel overwhelmed and not even remember some of what he asked. You may even suspect he does this to make you feel off-balance and somehow benefit from that.

Solution: Eventually he has to stop and take a breath! Remember: you have the information he needs, which means you have power in this situation. You have two good choices. First, answer the question *you* want. If he points out that you didn't answer another of his questions, respond with, "I'm happy to do that" and give your answer. Second, you can listen for the unifying trend in his questions and address that: "I think the larger issue you're getting at is …"

The Interrupter

Problem: She never lets you complete a thought before stopping you by asking another question or commenting on your—so far—less than complete answer. This gives you the impression she isn't interested in what you have to say and would rather listen to her own voice.

Solution: Of course what you'd really love to do is say, "If you'd just shut up for a minute, I'd give you the information you say you want!" Chances are, that's a little counterproductive. Try one of these two options instead. One: you can ignore the interruption. Keep talking and come back to answer the second question later. Don't talk over her, however, because that invites a shouting match—during which the other people in the room will feel they have to choose sides. Two: stop and listen patiently to the new question. Say, "I'll answer that in a minute," and then go on with, "As I was saying, …" Remember voice tone and quality here, and keep your voice calm. This helps you keep the power in and control of the situation. Whoever raises their voice first loses.

The Paraphraser

Problem: He unfairly and incorrectly restates what you just said. You think he may be doing this not because he misunderstood you, but because he has some other point he wants to make—and is willing to twist your words to do this.

Solution: Our first reaction is to get angry. You want to raise your voice and say, "You *know* that's not what I said!" Because you can only guess at his motivation, and don't want to have people choosing sides in this meeting, just restate your position carefully. Keep your voice calm and low, and say, "I guess I didn't make myself clear." Then make yourself clear. Do this as many times as you need to. Ultimately, there will be pressure from others in the room to stop this tactic, and public opinion will support you because you haven't lost your cool.

The Color Commentator

Problem: She makes a provocative statement without actually asking a question. Often this can come across as snarky, sarcastic or looking for a laugh—perhaps at your expense. You sense she may be doing this to get a reaction out of you, or call attention to herself.

Solution: Don't take the bait. Here are two good ways to respond. First, if it's a Q&A session, say, "Sorry, I don't think I understand your question," which invites her to ask a real one or bow out. Second, consider using bridging to get back to one of your main messages: "While I can't comment about that, what I *can* tell you is …"

The Silencer

Problem: He pauses for several seconds after you've finished answering a question. He looks at you—perhaps with raised eyebrows—as though giving you a chance to continue speaking. You've seen this a million times on TV "ambush interviews." It's usually used to make people feel so nervous about the silence that they start talking and say something they didn't plan on.

Solution: Often our predilection is to turn to the person and say, "Did that answer your question?" because the silence has made us uncomfortable enough to think we might not be doing a good job. If this is a confrontational situation, you've just given up your power. Try one of these two tactics instead. First, fill the void by bridging back to a key message. Try, "I'd be happy to give you a related example of how we ..." Second, if there's really nothing more to say, then just look at the questioner and smile.

The Investigator

Problem: She asks you for secrets or confidential information. You've seen this technique on every good cop/bad cop show on TV. These questions are often accompanied by a soft, conspiratorial voice tone, with the person leaning toward you, implying. "Just between the two of us ..." Her question also may be leading, indicating that she already knows the information and is just looking for confirmation—so you're really not sharing something that's secret.

Solution: This plays off the human condition of wanting others to believe we are "in the know" on something. Stick to the information it's OK for you to share and then bridge to one of your key messages. Try, "While I can't speak to *that*, what I can tell you is ..."

Sometimes It's What You Don't Say

Here's the toughest Q&A situation I've ever been in.

When I worked with the investor relations agency, one of my clients was developing a process for mixing "3-D sound." This meant no matter where the speakers were placed, the sound would appear to be coming from all around you. I visited the sound studios where the equipment was being tested, talked with the technicians, and the company looked legit.

The management team promised investors it would announce the first use of the new technology with a major recording artist by a certain date. As that time drew near, I began to press them for information so we would be ready to share it. They stopped taking my calls. In the days before email, I sent them faxes, telegrams and registered letters. I warned them of the big credibility problem we would have if they said nothing.

And they said nothing.

The day of the announcement came and went, with no word from the company. I resigned from the account.

Fast forward two years. I received a notice from the head of the Seattle bureau of the Securities and Exchange Commission (SEC). His office was investigating the former client for securities fraud. They subpoenaed all of my records and required me to attend a deposition.

Never having been "deposed" before, I met with our agency's attorney. He gave me the best advice: "Just answer the questions you are asked. Don't offer any opinions or additional information."

The day came. The SEC bureau chief sat at the end of the table. His court reporter—armed with a tape recorder—sat next to him. The attorney was at my side. I was hoping the chief would ask me the right questions so I could give him the information that would put this management team behind bars. We went painstakingly through nearly every document I sent to the bureau—including all of those faxes, telegrams and registered letters.

The chief looked at me at one point and said, "It must have been awfully frustrating to send all of these notices to the company, asking them to talk with investors, and get no reaction from them."

I gave him a rueful smile.

He got the message—but there was nothing on the official record. And he also got the information he needed to prosecute the company's leaders.

Knowing your audience really begins with knowing yourself. I'm a Listener and Doer. If I use that style with everyone, then I'll only persuade other Listener/Doers—which is a thin slice of the population. You've probably heard the line, "If all you have is a hammer, then everything is a nail." By watching others and noticing how they want to get and process information, I add new tools to my toolbox and can be more convincing with those who have other learning and communication styles. And by paying attention to how people ask me questions—and making sure I give them what they need while sharing what's important—I keep control of the Q&A session, increasing the chances that I will get what I want.

- Ninety-three percent of the information people get from you is nonverbal—through voice tone and quality. Make sure this matches the 7% they get from your messages.

- *Lookers* (75% of the population) think in images and pictures. Connect with them by giving them lots of eye contact and using "visual" words.

- *Listeners* (20%) think in words and sounds. Connect with them by not giving them too much eye contact and using "sound" words.

- *Feelers* (5%) think in feelings and kinesthetically. Connect with them by leaning in, feeling comfortable with occasional physical contact, and using "feeling" and "tactile" words.

- *Doers* are action oriented and like "to the point" communications. *Thinkers* are analytical and like all the details. *Feelers* are relationship oriented and like information presented with passion. *Creators* like abstractions presented in unusual ways.

- People asking questions of you will take many different approaches to get the information they want—or to score personal or professional points. Stay focused on not giving up control of the session, while sharing the messages you understand they want and need to know.

What to Do Now

Analyze Your Coworkers or Family Members Exercise

1. Pick four people who are important in your personal and/or professional life.

2. Determine how they think: Looker, Listener or Toucher. Analyze how they like to get information: Doer, Thinker, Feeler or Creator.

   a. _____

   b. _____

   c. _____

   d. _____

3. Choose one of them. Now that you know how he/she thinks and likes to get information, how will you change your approach to create better rapport?

   _____

   _____

   _____

   _____

Being Persuasive in Q&A Exercise

1. Pick one of the questions you created at the end of the last chapter.

    _____

    _____

2. How would an Omniscient Authority ask this question?

    _____

    _____

3. How would you answer it?

    _____

    _____

    _____

4. What might a Paraphraser say after hearing your answer?

    _____

    _____

    _____

5. What would you say to the Paraphraser?

_____

_____

_____

6. How will you handle an Interrupter who is peppering you with questions?

_____

_____

_____

7. How will you respond to a Silencer who is looking to make you feel uncomfortable and keep talking?

_____

_____

_____

Get Going

"There are risks and costs to action. But they are far less than the long range risks of comfortable inaction."
– John F. Kennedy

When it comes to persuasion, we can have many judgments about people. If you're a Looker, you may conjure the image of the stereotypically pushy used car salesman in a plaid suit. If you're a Listener, you may be hearing a fast-talking stockbroker doing a cold call, trying to get you to buy shares in some company you've never heard of. If you're a Toucher, you may imagine yourself in the presence of an insurance salesperson, warning you about all of the terrible things that will happen to your family if you die without protecting them with a policy.

We can have just as many judgments on persuasion itself. That it's about tricking people into agreeing with us. That it's about manipulating people into doing things they wouldn't ordinarily or don't want to do. That it's about conning them by making up information or inventing a situation.

As you have seen, persuasion is none of those things.

Getting others to do what we want is really about awareness. I've organized creating this mindset into the "Four Gets":

1. Get your brain back
2. Get clear on your goals
3. Get persuasive
4. Get communicating

There's nothing underhanded about any of these actions. Best of all, you don't have to change who you are to use them!

Get your brain back when you're in a stressful situation simply by asking, "What am I feeling?" That will take you from your survival brain—where you only have the three options of fight, flight or freeze—

into your emotional brain—where you have the five options of mad, sad, glad, hurt and afraid. And by making the choice that this situation is not going to ruin your day/ your career/ your life, you get your thinking brain back. Then you can come up with strategies to deal with the immediate and longer term situation. Because it's impossible to be persuasive when we are a deer in the headlights.

Get clear on your goals involves knowing what you want. That sounds so simple! But how many times have all of us sleepwalked through days, weeks or months without having a good sense of where we wished to go? This is like trying to find a house in a town that has no street signs or numbers or maps. You only discover it by chance and after doing a lot of wandering around. How much better it is to get your reticular activating system and subconscious involved, asking for what you want and letting your brain come up with ideas while your conscious mind is sleeping or doing something else?

Get persuasive involves knowing where people are in the Persuasion Cycle—and taking comfort in the idea that you only have to move them to the next step in it, rather than forcing a quantum leap. Now you don't have to take it personally when people resist a new idea you present: that's just how everyone's brain works. And you also have some useful strategies for moving others from resisting to listening to considering. This is the crucial "buy-in" part of the process—and if we don't get it right, the person we're trying to persuade will make us go back through it.

Get communicating has several moving pieces to it. First, you have to get your message right. This happens when you understand not only what *you* want to say, but who are the people you want to persuade and what *they* want and need to know. Second, you must know how to answer questions well. Instead of hoping people ask you the right questions, you now can use bridging, listing, flagging and hooking to make *every* question the right one. Third, you better understand the people you're dealing with. You can identify how they think (Lookers, Listeners and Touchers) and want information (Doers, Thinkers, Feelers and Creatives), and adjust your approach to sync with their preferences. And you know how to handle people who are trying to use Q&A for their own personal and professional reasons—rather than as an honest exchange of information.

Is your head ready to explode yet? Then take a deep breath and ask yourself, "What am I feeling?" (You *knew* that was coming, didn't you?)

You don't have to live in overwhelm. The best way to combat this is by doing something small. Write three goals for that big meeting you have coming up. Go back to the chapter on persuasion and do the exercises at the end (which you skipped and promised yourself you'd do later). Practice different ways to answer questions—and watch out for those different types of questioners. And as you start to see success with some strategies—and more people are doing what you want—then add a few more. Practice makes persuasive!

It took Fred—standing three feet away from me with a machete—to make me realize I needed to stop focusing on how I wanted the world to be, and start focusing on others to get what I want. You're smart enough to make this change without being held at knife point. So get going on getting others to do what you want!

About the Author

A year and a day, one broken nose and three cracked ribs later, Lynne Franklin got out of social work at Daniel Cottage. Fred and the other boys there had taught her everything she needed to know to survive in the business world. That started her on the path of discovering "how do you get others to do what you want?"

This professional journey took Lynne through positions as a reporter for a weekly banking magazine ("I knew when they said 'Fannie Mae' it wasn't the candy, but I had no clue!"), through a series of jobs with public and investor relations agencies and one corporation, to starting Lynne Franklin Wordsmith—her corporate communications and marketing practice—in 1993.

Along the way, Lynne turned into a neuroscience nerd. She studies how the brain works, how this affects the choices people make, and how to create communications that move their minds to action. ("I want to be more than just another pretty phrase.")

Today, Lynne works with CEOs, CFOs, entrepreneurs and business leaders on how to create and share messages that are attractive to their customers, employees, investors and the media. She also is a professional speaker and trainer on persuasive business communication strategies. Lynne is committed to helping people laugh, learn, and get strategies they can use right away to solve their problems and get what they want.

Learn more about Lynne at www.linkedin.com/in/LynneFranklin, and http://twitter.com/LynneFranklin or contact her directly at lynne@yourwordsmith.com. And **don't forget to download your gift**— *Something Funny about Business Communication: 12 Oddball Theories and 38 Tips for Getting What You Want on the Job*—and sign up for Lynne's monthly *In Communicado* neuroscience and communication newsletter at www.yourwordsmith.com.